Stories to hear with your Heart

FOR EVERYONE WHO BELIEVES IN MIRACLES.
AND FOR EVERYONE WHO DOESN'T.

SARAH KARMELY

Copyright © 2014 by Sarah Karmely.
All rights reserved.

No part of this book may be reproduced or transmitted in any form or by any means, electronic or mechanical, including photocopying, recording, or by any information storage and retrieval system, without permission in writing from the copyright owner.

ISBN: 978-0-9861034-0-7

Printed in the United States of America

To schedule speaking events and order additional copies, contact the author at:
Website: SarahKarmely.com
Cell: 917-770-1664
Email: sarahkarmely@aol.com

Contents

Foreword 7

Acknowledgements 9

Sponsors 11

Encounters With the Rebbe 13
Introduction   14
She Was the Rebbe's Child   14
An Uncommon Divorce   15
What Daughter?   16
Davening for a Shidduch in the Rebbe's Room   17
He Had an Allergy to Rabbis   17
How Did He Know?   19
A Kaddish for Their Mothers   20
Two Sets of Triplets and an Aunt   21
Vignettes in a Vehicle on Tisha B'Av   22
The Yarmulke Fell Off   24
The Tanya Saved Him From Death   25
The Test That Never Happened   27

Meeting Your Mate 29
We Were Already Married in the Womb   30
The Money in the Gemara   32
The Splitting of the Sea and Shidduchim   33
Do You Want to Marry Me?   34
Passion Is for the Movies: True or False?   35
Check, Check and Check Again   37
Important Message for Singles   38

Stories About Marriage 39
Be Careful What You Wish For   40
Marriage Is What You Make of It   43
Shoes and Sensitivity   43
"Love and Marriage Go Together Like a Horse and Carriage."
Do They?   44
What's So Special About the Ring Finger?   45

The Hunchback in the Mirror	46
Persian Betrothals	47
The Rebbe's Marriage Advice	48
Disposable Society, Disposable Spouses	50
Fire And Ice	51
Communication Tips From the Ten Commandments	51
Get Your Own Tea – Or Not	52
Are You a Willow or an Oak?	53
Even a Bad Marriage Is Bashert	54
Sorry, I Have to Hang Up Now	55
An Onion on Marriage	56
Thank You Avraham Fried	57
Top Twelve Tips To Tranquility	59
Two Eyes, Two Ears and Your Mother-In-Law	63
Please Give My Husband Parnasah	65

Stories About Mikvah 67

The Mystique of the Mikvah I	68
The Mystique of the Mikvah II	70
A Hole in the Ice	73
"I Think My Husband Is Cheating On Me"	75
The Four Mysterious Women at the Mikvah	76
Niddah Is Not a Mitzvah	78

Stories About Jewish Women. 81

What I Said to the American Jewish Book Council About Jewish Women	82
Three Mitzvos for a Meaningful Life	83
The Chassidic Connotations of the Three C's	85
The Rebbetzin Places an Order	87
Have Faith Will Travel	88
Just an 'Ordinary' Jewish Woman	89
Miriam, the Prophetess of Jerusalem	90
It Happened at Bergdorf-Goodman	94
Miryam the Beautiful	96

On the Road Again. 103

Author's Note:	104
A Message From Gate 64	104
An Airport, a Defibrillator and a Kiddush Hashem	105
Rediscovering My Dad	106
Inspiration From an Inscription	108

Notes Aboard an El-Al Flight   108
Eliyahu Hanavi's Appearance in the Channel Islands   109
The California Couple   111
My Makeup Bag and the TSA Agent   113
Four Stories, Seven Days and Nine Speeches in South Africa   114
Coming Full Circle in Milan   118

Simcha: Don't Worry. Be Happy. **121**
What is the Rooster Crowing About?   122
Enter Simcha, Exit Stress   123

Stories About Mezuzah **125**
The Wow Factor   126
The Smashed Mezuzah Masterpiece   127

Stories About the Baal Shem Tov **129**
What's in a Name?   130
Rebirth   130
They Passed the Test   131
A Radical Concept Brings Joy   132
When Your Teachings Spread Out   133
Miraculous Missions   134
The Power of Baruch Hashem   135

Letters **137**

Glossary **141**

Foreword

Writing is hard work. I suspect that even best-selling authors, or should I say particularly best-selling authors, would agree with me. Writing a book is a full time, ever-present, all-consuming task; it takes over your life as surely as a newborn infant. I use this analogy precisely because the two have the same rewards.

The minor inconveniences of taking care of a new baby pale in significance to the incomparable pleasure and Nachas we gain with that first smile. The hard work involved in the writing of a book dissolves instantaneously upon the first positive response from a reader.

This is even truer when writing a book based on Torah teachings. Words that come from the heart enter the heart and the words from our Rabbis and Sages not only enter the heart, they penetrate it and transform our lives forever.

I was very pleased with the feedback from my first book *Words to Hear with Your Heart* and happy that I had written it. Once it was published, I figured that's that, my work was now done. But G-d had other plans for me because during my speaking engagements, so many people told me new and wonderful stories about the Rebbe, about miracles and Hashgacha Protis, that the idea of writing a second book began to incubate in my mind.

I wrote a note to the Rebbe that I was thinking about writing a new book, and I placed it at the Ohel. Just a few moments later,

I happened to glance up at the screen that plays the Rebbe's talks 24/7. The Rebbe was giving out dollars and asked one of the people in line, "When are you writing your new book?"

Of course I realized that this was hardly a coincidence but it took three more times when I went to the Ohel and the exact same sequence showed up on the screen, before I actually said, "Yes, I finally got the message," and began production on this book. Thank you Rebbe.

The actual writing of the book however was taking a toll on me and I was feeling quite overwhelmed. I was busy taking care of my family, going on B"H many speaking engagements and other commitments that left me with absolutely no spare time. I felt that perhaps I had undertaken a task that was unnecessary. I had already written one successful book, thank G-d, did I really need another? Did anyone?

Hashem sends us messages in subtle but very direct ways and just as these thoughts were causing me doubts, Hashem gave me my answer. I was attending a family wedding when an attractive young woman approached me. "Mrs. Karmely, I am so thrilled to meet you," she said with a sweet smile, "because I want to thank you for writing your book. I want you to know that it really helped me in so many ways. I even bought your book for my friends and they told me that it made a huge difference in their lives as well."

She also asked if I would speak to a group of her friends, which I agreed to with pleasure. I told her that her words of encouragement could not have come at a more propitious moment because I was in the process of writing a new book and " I have serious misgivings about whether it's a worthwhile thing to do. Your words are a sign to me from Hashem that I should 'stay calm and carry on.' Thank you."

Thank you Hashem for your timely signs and signals and for steering me in the right direction. I pray that this book will also speak to the heart of the reader and open it to receive Hashem's blessings even more fully. I hope that it will inspire the reader to grow in Torah and Mitzvos and to disseminate Yiddishkeit in their surroundings.

Please note that most names have been changed to protect privacy.

May we all be Zoche to spread the wellsprings of Torah and Chassidus in order to bring the greatest Simcha of all, the coming of Mashiach Tzidkeinu. May he come even before you finish reading this book.

Acknowledgements

I would first like to give thanks to HaKadosh Boruch Hu for His great chessed, which is undeserved.

There are many people whom I wish to thank for this book. My first acknowledgment is to our dear Rebbe, Rabbi Menachem Mendel Schneerson of saintly memory, who encouraged all of us to reach for greater heights and to never accept defeat in our task of bringing increased holiness into the world.

My second thank you goes to my life partner, my closest friend and the love of my life: my dear husband Benyamin. He is surely a Tzaddik because it is not easy being married to me. I am so often away from home, traveling around the world teaching and counseling. Benyamin says good-humoredly that he is often asked whether he is related to Sarah Karmely. He actually enjoys saying he is my husband. Benyamin has grown tremendously in his Yiddishkeit, showing a perseverance that is remarkable. He has taught me to be patient and to appreciate baby steps. He has morphed from objecting to my being a Lubavitcher Chassid and teacher to actually being proud of my work. I am even more proud to be his wife.

To our dear children: David Yecheskel and Chanah Devorah, Esther and Mordechai, Daniella Miriam and Elroyi Benyamin. Thank you for giving me more Nachas than I deserve. I am humbled to be your mother. You are my world.

Of course I have to mention our precious grandchildren may they all be well, they are the light of our lives. For them alone I would say Dayenu, but we were recently additionally blessed with a sweet great-grandson. I am infinitely grateful to Hakadosh Baruch Hu for granting us these holy Neshamot.

Thank you to my cover, graphic and layout team: Nechama Marcus, Rabbi Zalman Friedman and Yaakov Lipsker. You all did a fantastic job. Thank you to my photographer, Devorah Goldstein. Thank you Rishe Deitsch for your proofreading and constant loving care.

And last but certainly not least, a very special thank you goes to my editor, Fay Kranz Greene. Fay, without you this book would not be, and I owe you a huge Yasher Koach. Your talents are amazing, as is the rest of your special family, whom I esteem and admire.

Sponsors

I wish to gratefully thank the following sponsors who made the publication of this book possible. May you all be Zoche to receive endless blessings from Hashem and may you merit that this book be the catalyst for positive change in the lives of all who read it.

The Dafna Family

Yitzchok and Julie Gniwisch

Pari LeVian (Yaffa bat Miriam)

The Mehdizade Family

In loving memory of Mrs. Chana Breina bas Yitzchok Dovid Sholom a"h

Encounters with

The Rebbe

> **Introduction**
> What is it about a story that enthralls us? From the cradle years to the golden years, everyone loves a good story and the best ones are about our holy Tzaddikim. The following stories about the Rebbe are sure to make your Neshama smile.

She Was the Rebbe's Child

I recently attended a friend's wedding and when I went to wish the mother Mazel Tov, I could not help but comment how taken I was with her daughter. The Kallah looked so refined and modest, I was sure she was an especially lovely girl.

"She is the Rebbe's Bracha," the mother whispered to me. "When I was in my last month of pregnancy with her, the doctors told me that the baby was in the transverse position and they would have to turn her in-utero. I told the doctor that we would have to ask for the Rebbe's Bracha first."

"They were adamant and said that I will most definitely need a C-section if we don't turn the baby now, because it could not be born naturally in this position. When I told this to the Rebbe, he firmly and unequivocally told us 'do not turn the baby, leave everything as is.' Which we did."

"As the doctors expected, when the time came for delivery, she was still transverse and they *did* have to do a C-section. After the surgery the doctor came over to me ashen-faced. 'We don't know who your rabbi is, but he must be very special because as we began the surgery, we saw immediately that your baby was in a dangerous position. Had we attempted to turn her in-utero, we would have snapped her neck. We are very grateful that your rabbi didn't let us do it.'"

This was clearly the Rebbe's Bracha and she was the only one of her children to be born by C-section, as her subsequent births were all natural. The grateful mother felt that her daughter was also the Rebbe's daughter. "That's why you think she's special."

An Uncommon Divorce

Divorce is practically unheard of in the Persian Mashadi community. Marriages are arranged by the family and there are rarely skeletons in the closet, because everybody knows everybody else's family tree, going back many generations.

However, sometimes the unthinkable happens and tragedy strikes. Such was the case with Shulamit, a young, attractive newlywed bride from a family that was very well respected in the community. Barely two weeks after the wedding, her parents had to rescue her from her husband. He was mentally ill and had been beating her severely. Somehow, his family had managed to keep their son's illness a secret.

Shulamit's parents of course arranged for a quick divorce, but the tragic plight of their young and innocent daughter made life unbearable for them. Her mother took it especially hard. After a year had passed, Shulamit's mother approached me with tears streaming down her face and asked what she could do to "atone for her sins." The poor woman felt that Hashem was punishing Shulamit because of her sins. "What can I do to change this situation?" she asked me.

I suggested that she should write to the Rebbe as soon as possible and ask him for a Bracha. A few days later, we went together to 770 and waited outside the Rebbe's room. As he came out to Daven Mincha, we gave him the letter. The answer was quick in coming. The Rebbe's advice was for the mother to start keeping Taharat Hamishpacha "according to the Shulchan Aruch," the Code of Jewish Law.

At that time, the Persian-language Shulchan Aruch had not yet been printed and because the mother did not speak any other language, I served as her translator and we studied the laws of Mikvah together. She and her husband began to observe Taharat Hamishpacha scrupulously as the Rebbe had recommended. Not long thereafter, Shulamit was introduced to a fine young man whom she eventually married, and they were blessed with four beautiful children.

Every time I meet Shulamit or her mother, I am reminded again of how many lives were changed by the Rebbe's guidance and how keeping Taharat Hamishpacha can work miracles.

What Daughter?

The Rebbe had long ago advised me to reach out to the women in the Persian Jewish communities because I am Persian and speak Farsi fluently. He felt that they would respond more positively to someone who speaks their language. Of course the Rebbe was right and I have Baruch Hashem seen extraordinary results.

My talks have taken me to Persian Jewish communities around the world. The one in Los Angeles is probably among the largest, so I find myself visiting that lovely city quite frequently.

On a recent trip I spoke to a very large group of women and girls. After my talk, a woman approached me with a pretty young lady at her side and without any preamble whatsoever said, "This is my daughter who is my gift, my Bracha, from the Rebbe." Of course I was intrigued and wanted to hear the whole story and here it is exactly as she told it to me that evening.

"My husband and I were married for several years and were not able to have a child. After many attempts and procedures, all to no avail, someone suggested to me that I go to the Lubavitcher Rebbe for Sunday dollars and ask for his blessing. We were not at all observant but we were desperate, so I went. I stood in line for what seemed like hours, but finally my turn came to stand before the Rebbe."

"As I looked into his penetrating eyes, my emotions overwhelmed me and I couldn't talk or ask him for anything. To my utter embarrassment, I burst into tears. The Rebbe didn't say anything, he just handed me a dollar and wished me "good news." As I turned to go, he called me back, handed me another dollar and said, "This dollar is for your daughter."

"I had not managed to tell the Rebbe that we didn't have any children and it didn't seem to me that the Rebbe was giving me a Bracha for children. I really thought the Rebbe had made a mistake. Why had he given me a dollar for a daughter that I did not have? I admit I left feeling rather despondent."

"My disappointment however turned into great joy because *exactly* nine months later, I gave birth to our beautiful daughter. And here she is now, our beautiful gift from the Rebbe."

Davening for a Shidduch in the Rebbe's Room

I always like to ask couples how they met, because more often than not, I can see the concept of Bashert at work. Batsheva recently told me the story of how she met her husband. She had managed to leave Iran more than 15 years ago and moved to the U.S. Although she is a very personable and attractive woman, marriage had eluded her. Every prospective Shidduch seemed to go nowhere. Batsheva was slowly losing hope that she would ever find her match.

Last year, on the Rebbe's Yahrzeit, she happened to be in Crown Heights, when a friend told her that the Rebbe's office was open and everyone was welcome to go inside. "Why don't you go and say a prayer there?" her friend suggested.

Batsheva had never met the Rebbe and of course had never been in that room. When she walked inside, she was awestruck by the holiness that she felt. Batsheva has the strong Emunat Tzaddikim - the belief in saintly people - of the Sephardim. Tears welled up in her eyes and she allowed them to flow freely as she poured out her heart to Hashem and to the Rebbe. She closed her eyes and prayed from the depths of her being that her Bashert would soon be revealed.

She stayed in that position for a little while longer and when she finally opened her eyes, she felt a little guilty that she had taken up more than her allotted time. But when she looked at the clock in the room, she could not believe her eyes, and rubbed them to make sure that she wasn't imagining it. The time had barely moved; she had been in there for less than three minutes, although she was sure it had been at least twenty.

Batsheva left the Rebbe's room with a lightness of heart and a happiness that she had not experienced before. Exactly one month later, she celebrated her engagement.

He Had an Allergy to Rabbis

We know that blessings often come from unexpected sources. What we don't realize however is that the Bracha sometimes comes through the quiet intervention of a Rebbe. How do I know? This particular story occurred with me, but I'm sure it happened to many others.

Years ago, I was in charge of a Talmud Torah, an after-school program for the children in our community who attended Public Schools. My ultimate goal for the Talmud Torah was for it to be so successful that it would have to close – because all of the kids would enroll in full time Jewish Day Schools.

Pretty quickly I began to realize that this might take a while. Everything was difficult. There was no staff, no money and I had to do everything by myself. The president of our community was a very good man, but not too fond of Orthodox Judaism. He used to tell me that he was "allergic" to rabbis and didn't value a Talmud Torah school at all.

However, he was also the only person who could authorize any innovations or new programs and I knew I had to "soften him up" if the school was to succeed. It was quite a struggle; one step forward and ten steps backwards. I was frustrated but determined to keep trying. One day to my great surprise he called me into his office and encouraged me not to give up on the school and to continue teaching the classes. He even asked me to schedule classes three times per week instead of the two we were already doing. And for the icing on the cake, he said that money was no object and that I could purchase whatever we needed.

To say I was incredulous would be an understatement. I needed to find out why he had such a sudden change of mind and with my characteristic Chutzpa, I asked him point blank. His answer was even more surprising.

He told me that night after night he had been having the same vivid dream. He dreamt that the Lubavitcher Rebbe was encouraging him to "help Mrs. Karmely run the school." When this continued for several more nights, he realized that these were not ordinary dreams but personal and insistent messages that were being directed to him by a very holy man. The dreams worked their magic and the president made a complete 360-degree turnabout and became one of our most enthusiastic supporters. Without his help the school would never have gotten off the ground, so the Rebbe had to step in and find a way to save this vitally important program.

I am so grateful that I pressed him for an explanation about why he changed his mind. Otherwise I would never have known that it was motivated by the Rebbe quietly helping his children. Those children are adults today, but they still recall how good they felt when I would take them to the Rebbe. They often tell me that they remember the Rebbe would thank me for the photos I gave him of the school activities.

I have a video of many of the people that I brought with me to the Rebbe in those years. In many of them I can see the Rebbe saying, "Please help Mrs. Karmely in her work." I can't help but smile.

You know, the experts say that the people in our lives might forget what we did for them, but they will always remember how we made them *feel*. That was the essence of the Rebbe who cared for all of us like a father and we will never forget that feeling.

P.S. The "allergy" that the shul president had to rabbis has now definitely been cured.

How Did He Know?

Rabbi Nasirov, a Bukharian rabbi from a Sephardic congregation in Queens, used to encourage his brides to attend my Kallah classes, even though their command of English was sometimes limited. These lovely young Russian girls had strong family ties and were mostly from Samarkand or Tashkent.

During one of our classes, when I mentioned the Rebbe's name, I noticed that Tanya was smiling and her face was lit up in recognition. After class she came over and said that she and her mother were fortunate to have left Russia during those days when being openly Jewish was dangerous and that she had personally met the Rebbe when they immigrated to New York.

"One Sunday afternoon my mother took me to 770 and after standing in line for a while, the Rebbe gave each of us a dollar bill. Suddenly he turned to my mom and said in Russian: 'And these are for the others in your family who will come to the United States and it should be very soon.'" The Rebbe then handed her mother an additional *six* crisp dollar bills.

They were stunned. Her father had refused to leave his elderly mother in Russia so he and the rest of her family, six people, had stayed behind. She and her mother had come alone with the intention that they would do everything possible to be reunited. Her mother had not mentioned this to the Rebbe and had not said a word about the rest of the family.

"How did the Rebbe know that we left my father, my grandmother and my four brothers back in Russia?" Tanya asked me incredulously. I had no answer for her, but the Bracha of the Rebbe was soon fulfilled and miraculously all of them were able to leave Russia and, when the time came, they all attended Tanya's wedding.

A Kaddish for Their Mothers

Eliahu Golran, a traditional Persian Jew and my husband's dear cousin, lives in Milan, Italy. Although he is not a Torah scholar he has more than compensated for it by his piety, conscientious Davening and humble faith in Tzaddikim and is very respected by his family and friends.

One of his visits to our family happened to coincide with the Yahrzeit of his beloved mother. My husband took him to 770 so that he could daven and say Kaddish with the Rebbe's Minyan. Our cousin was unaware that during those days, the Rebbe was leading the Davening and saying Kaddish for the Yahrtzeit of his holy mother, Rebbetzin Chana of righteous memory. As the Rebbe started to say Kaddish, it became silent in the room, but suddenly everyone could hear Eliahu loudly, clearly and carefully saying Kaddish for *his* mother.

The men who were Davening next to him tried to quiet him down, but Eliahu did not realize that he was doing anything wrong. He was unaware that Chassidim who need to say Kaddish do not recite it together with the Rebbe, they attend another Minyan afterwards. The innocent visitor therefore ignored their requests and continued his Kaddish in a loud voice.

Almost immediately, however, the Rebbe himself turned to the people who were shushing Eliahu and with a stern glance he stopped them. The Rebbe motioned to our cousin to continue and waited respectfully while Eliahu recited the Kaddish. Only after he was done did the Rebbe begin his Kaddish for the Rebbetzin Chana.

After Mincha, the Rebbe smiled at Eliahu and nodded his head approvingly. The Rebbe turned a potentially embarrassing moment into one of respect and acceptance and from that day on, Eliahu became a devoted admirer of the Rebbe. His inherent spark was ignited and his Yiddishkeit grew in leaps and bounds.

Two Sets of Triplets and an Aunt

I recently heard a story at a very special Simcha. It was a Kiddush in celebration of the Bar Mitzvah of two special young men - part of a set of triplets, two boys and a girl, all of them born as a result of a Bracha from the Rebbe.

The parents of these triplets had been married for many years but had not been blessed with children. It happened that they were invited to 770 to see the Rebbe at a special evening for Chabad supporters. They attended together with another couple, married for seven years and also childless. After speaking to the Rebbe for a few minutes, the Rebbe gave each of the wives three dollars and also gave them a Bracha for children. He told the women to be extremely meticulous in their observance of the Mitzvah of Taharat Hamishpacha. Within the year both couples gave birth to triplets! They all became totally observant and embraced the Chabad way of life, always giving credit to the Rebbe for their six miracle babies.

Back to the Bar Mitzvah: I was seated next to a woman and her daughter and we began talking about the miracle of the birth of the Bar Mitzvah boys. The woman told me that her husband had an equally amazing story with the Rebbe and brought him over to the table so that he could tell it to me firsthand.

Here is his story. "I was not raised as a Lubavitcher," he began, "but I once merited to receive a Bracha from the Rebbe for my sick aunt and I will always be indebted to him." He told me that as a young man, he studied in the Yeshiva in Lakewood and was once invited to 770 by a young Chabad Rabbi who was teaching there. "I had no intention of going," he recalls, "but all my friends seemed to be interested, so I went along."

They told him he would be there during Kos Shel Bracha, the sips of wine that the Rebbe poured from his cup for all those present. "I hadn't expected to actually meet the Rebbe," he told me, "but I realized this might be a good opportunity to ask for a blessing for my very sick aunt." The poor woman had been diagnosed with terminal pancreatic cancer, had an ongoing raging fever and was told she had only about a month to live.

It was way past midnight when the young man's turn came to stand before the Rebbe. Shaking and nervous, he gathered the courage to ask for a blessing for his aunt, saying her name and her mother's name. The Rebbe looked at him and said "Refuah Shleimah, a speedy recovery and good news." He went away feeling hopeful and for some reason checked his watch; it was exactly 2:00 in the morning. The following day, as soon as he awoke he called the hospital to inquire about his aunt. "I got the chills when I was told that her fever had broken and she was getting stronger. I asked the nurse if she had any idea what time the fever had broken and she said it happened at approximately 2:00."

He told me that I could check his story out if I wanted to (I didn't) because it was written up in medical journals and had been studied by several doctors who could not explain her complete and sudden recovery. Ten years later, the young man's aunt was diagnosed with a heart illness and she asked her nephew to go to the Rebbe for another Bracha. Such was her faith and trust in a Tzaddik. She recovered from that illness too and continued to live a good life for another twenty-five years.

Vignettes in a Vehicle on Tisha B'Av

It is a Sephardic custom to visit the resting places of Tzaddikim on Tisha B'av, which commemorates the destruction of the first and second Temples.

This year I took a large group of Iranian Jews, three carloads full, to the Rebbe's Ohel. The car I was driving was filled with women who were very excited about the trip. They had fond memories of going with me to the Rebbe for dollars years ago and three of the women shared their personal stories about those dollars as we were driving to the Ohel. And now I am sharing them with you:

The Decree 'Passed Over'

Dina was widowed at a young age and was left with four children. One of her daughters, Hadassah, was of marriageable age and there were several prospective Shidduchim knocking on their door. None of them however turned out to be the right one. After a while things began to look up for Hadassah again and she was dating a man who seemed extremely promising. To everyone's disappointment, however, he soon ended the relationship.

Her mother decided to ask the Rebbe for a Bracha and on the following Sunday, she boarded the bus that I had arranged and set off with a prayer that her daughter's Mazel would change for the better.

When it was her turn to receive her dollar, she broke down and tearfully told the Rebbe that she had a daughter who needed to get married, but her Mazel seemed to be blocked. The Rebbe smiled at her, waved his hand and said, "Passover." I explained to Dina, who speaks only Farsi, what the word "passover" means. She decided that the Rebbe waved his hand to assure that any negative decree should indeed *pass over*.

Dina's pure and simple faith was a vehicle for the Rebbe's Bracha and the following Pesach, Hadassah indeed became a Kallah and is now happily married with a lovely family.

Hannah's Happiness

Hannah, another passenger in our car, also had an incident she wanted to share. "The last time I went to the Rebbe, I had just found out that I was pregnant and had not yet told anyone. When it was my turn, the Rebbe gave me a dollar and then, with a wonderful smile, he gave me another one and said, 'This is for your child.' I kept this special dollar until my baby was born and I was secure and confident that everything would turn out well. Thank G-d, it did."

Rachel's Resurgence

Rachel was in the car behind us and also had a story about the Rebbe. Here it is.

It was a mystery to everyone why Rachel could not find a Shidduch. A vivacious, attractive girl with a warm personality and a great sense of humor, Rachel tried in vain to find her Bashert. She was set up on many dates but they never worked out. No matter what she did, nothing and no one materialized and eventually she just gave up and despaired of ever getting married.

One Shabbos, after Rachel poured out her heart to me and explained her difficult situation, I asked if she would like to join a group whom I was taking to see the Rebbe. Although Rachel was not a Chassid of the Rebbe and not yet observant, I didn't need to ask twice. She eagerly accepted and joined us with a new glimmer of hope in her heart.

We waited in line for what seemed like a long time that day and when Rachel finally came face to face with the Rebbe, she tried to ask for a Bracha but was so overcome with emotion, she just stood there and cried. I quietly mentioned to the Rebbe that she was there to ask for a Shidduch. The Rebbe said 'Amen,' smiled at Rachel and gave her another dollar.

Subsequently Rachel received an answer to a letter that she had written to the Rebbe in which she asked for advice on what she could do in order to find her Bashert. The Rebbe's reply was, "Your conduct should be according to the Shulchan Aruch."

This was a huge step for Rachel and I encouraged her to listen to the Rebbe's advice and live a Torah-true life. But Rachel was too fearful to change her lifestyle right then. She was convinced that she could only observe Shabbat if she were married. "Right now in my single state, how can I stay off the phone or not go out with my friends on Saturday or not eat in the same restaurants they do?"

So although she was a regular guest in our home for Shabbat and enjoyed and appreciated the Shabbat experience, Rachel could not commit.

After a while with no great marriage prospects in sight, I begged her to try and change her circle of friends and try to hang out with a more observant crowd. She tentatively started keeping some Mitzvos and stopped going to the mall on Shabbos. (I had told her to try whatever worked.)

After a few months, Rachel very hesitantly attended a Singles Shabbaton. While there she met a wonderful young man from a Chassidishe background. As soon as they were introduced, both knew instinctively that they were destined for each other. Two months later Rachel's dream came true; they got married and began building an observant Jewish home.

Rachel is convinced that had she listened to the Rebbe's advice, she would have been married earlier. Her husband agrees and teasingly says that she kept him waiting too long.

The Yarmulke Fell Off

Amir Rashtian is a wonderful Persian gentleman from Great Neck who is a G-d-fearing Jew and a great philanthropist. Amir loves to tell the story of how he first met the Rebbe.

One afternoon he decided to go to 770 for the very first time. It was just before Mincha and he waited in the lobby where the Rebbe would soon pass, hoping to catch a glimpse of the great leader he had heard so much about.

The Rebbe came out of his room and Amir found himself face to face with this holy man. It is a custom among Persian Jews to kiss the hand of a rabbi or an elder as a sign of respect. Overcome with awe, Amir impulsively and reverently took the Rebbe's hand and kissed it.

As he was bending over, the yarmulke that was perched precariously on his head fell to the floor.

Before anyone could think what to do, the Rebbe had already bent down, retrieved the fallen yarmulke and placed it gently back on Amir's head. The Rebbe gave him a radiant smile and proceeded to the shul for Mincha.

Amir told us that several people offered to buy the yarmulke from him that day but to him it was priceless and he would never sell it. "The Rebbe taught me a valuable lesson, that my head should be covered at all times," says Amir. "So I put that yarmulke away to be used only for special occasions and for everyday I now wear a good, sturdy and non-slippery one." The Rebbe bent down to retrieve a yarmulke and it brought another Jew closer to Yiddishkeit.

The Rebbe always referred to every Jew as a "believer" and would use the term "not *yet* Frum" when referring to a non-observant Jew. The Rebbe taught us to use positive words at all times.

The Prophet Amos said, "The day is coming when there will be a hunger and thirst; not for bread and water but for G-dliness." Are we not seeing that thirst for spirituality throughout the world right now?

The Tanya Saved Him From Death

When the Ayatollah Khomeini (Yemach Shemo) came to power in Iran, he enacted strict edicts against anyone and anything that could be perceived as aiding Zionism and the State of Israel.

The Taliban claimed that their enemies were the Zionists, not necessarily the Jews or the Jewish religion. What a lie that turned out to be, but the following miraculous story is one exception to the rule.

Rabbi Yedidya Ezrachian, a Sephardic rabbi in Teheran, had narrowly escaped death when the Ayatollah came to power. A scholarly, saintly man of great Yirat Shamayim, Rabbi Ezrachian was also a Chassid of the Rebbe.

Just as the revolution was taking its toll on the Jews in Iran, this brave Rav was in the process of translating the Tanya into Farsi

(Persian). This was a dangerous task, because anything in Hebrew would be construed as being "Zionistic," a sin punishable by death.

One night, Rabbi Ezrachian was hard at work at his desk in the shul,

Rabbi Yedidya Ezrachian

when suddenly there was a loud, insistent banging on the door. He heard the unmistakable shouts of the fanatical Taliban police, violent Moslem clerics, who were always looking for any excuse to spill Jewish blood in order to prove their loyalty to the Imam. Any excuse would have sufficed for these hoodlums whose zeal is legendary, deadly and uncompromising.

Rabbi Ezrachian raced to the door, his heart pounding so loudly he was sure they could hear. His office was filled with the receipts of money that people in his shul had donated and all of them were earmarked for Israel. He had intended to destroy them in a few days but hadn't done it yet. Now if these receipts were found, it would be considered aiding the enemy and he would surely be shot on the spot.

Numbly he stood there as the screaming mob of clerics burst in. They immediately started to pull open doors, closets, files, anything they could get their hands on. He held his breath; any minute now they would find the documents. He was staring certain death in the face.

Rabbi Ezrachian automatically recited the 'Vidui,' the prayer before death. As he prepared to meet his maker, he felt himself getting weaker and with his last bit of strength, he prayed to Hashem. "Please let the merit of the holy Tanya protect me."

At that moment, the chief of the clerics pounced on one of the many Sifrei Tanya that there were in the office. He leafed through it and then asked Rabbi Ezrachian in a cruel venomous tone, "and what is this?" "It is a very holy book and I am translating it into Farsi," the trembling Rabbi Ezrachian stammered. The cleric proceeded to open the Tanya and randomly selected a page. "Translate this for me exactly as it is written," he commanded. By Divine

Providence, the page was from Shaar HaYichud V'Haemunah, the treatise that commands us to love G-d.

Rabbi Ezrachian translated it faithfully and after a few minutes they told him to stop. All the policemen/clerics were now listening quietly with great awe. Their leader then reverently took the Tanya, gently touched it to his eyes and kissed it. (Persians have this custom to show respect.) "A book like this is something we all need," he said. "We do not have to search any longer, it's obvious this man reveres Allah." They exempted Rabbi Ezrachian from any further forms of persecution. A paper was issued to allow the Rabbi to continue translating his holy book. Then they left as suddenly as they had come.

Rabbi Ezrachian fell to the ground in a faint. When he regained consciousness, he could not grasp the fact that he was still alive. They had not discovered the receipts, or the letters from Israel. Even *just one* of those documents would have meant certain death and he was in possession of dozens of them. The holy Sefer Tanya had indeed saved his life.

Note: Rabbi Ezrachian managed to escape from Iran and moved to Great Neck, Long Island, where I had the Zchut to interview him and hear this remarkable story.

The Test That Never Happened

The woman's voice on the phone was urgent and worried: "I have to see you immediately." I told her to come right over and she told me her story. "I already have two little girls thank G-d, and for the past eight years I have been trying to conceive again without success. Now, after all this time, I am finally pregnant. The problem is that at my last routine exam, the doctors found an abnormality that looks suspicious. They warned me that at my age it could be any number of serious birth defects and they urged me to undergo amniocentesis."

I asked her what she would do if the results were G-d forbid positive. At that question, she broke down. "My husband told me that I must have the amnio and if it's positive, he definitely wants me to have an abortion. He even threatened me with divorce if I don't do as he wants. He can't handle the idea of an imperfect child and refuses to even discuss it."

I asked her to give me a day to think about the answer and I immediately went to the Rebbe's Ohel and wrote a note describing the situation. I wrote that this couple already had marital problems and now, not only was their marriage being threatened, but the life of their baby was at stake as well. It was a very serious situation.

I asked the Rebbe for a Bracha and left the Ohel feeling confident and hopeful.

The next day I called the woman and urged her to take another simple blood test before she even considered doing the amnio. "But I already had the blood test," she argued, "and it was suspicious." I told her she had nothing to lose and it was her right to be retested. I suggested she just be firm with her doctor.

Thank G-d she agreed and underwent the same blood test as before. I soon received another call from her, but this time she was crying tears of joy. "The doctors are in shock," she said. "They think there must have been a terrible mistake, because the tests show that the baby is 100% healthy. There is no problem and therefore no need for me to have the amnio."

Of course there was no mistake. It was the Rebbe helping his children. Thank you Rebbe, You will never abandon us because a shepherd never abandons his flock.

This story has an even happier ending. Nine months later the pregnancy that caused them so much worry resulted in the birth of a healthy baby boy. The couple were ecstatic, especially the husband. Iranian men love their daughters, but they really value sons and his dream was to have a boy. "We know that the Rebbe is still watching over us," they said.

Stories about

Meeting your Mate

We Were Already Married in the Womb

Read the following paragraph carefully because to me this sums up everything we need to know about marriage.

If you are married, you probably believe that you personally chose your spouse all by yourself. You are certain that you made the choice without coercion and with your own free will. But it's just not true!

The Talmud tells us that forty days before a child is even conceived, a Heavenly voice announces the name of the person whom this unborn child is destined to marry. The amniotic fluid that cradles us in the womb already contains an allusion to our future spouse, to our Bashert. The souls of husband and wife share a connection even before their parents have conceived them. This is powerful stuff, and it means that the person we are married to is the one we are supposed to be married to; the one that Hashem Himself chose for us.

If this is true, you might be asking yourself, why does the Torah permit divorce?

To find the answer, we have to do a little Talmudic disputation; cue the singsong tone. We can actually learn about a good marriage from the laws governing divorce. In fact, it is strange but true that in the order of the Talmud the Halachot of divorce come before those of marriage.

The Talmud states that the altar in the Beit Hamikdash would shed tears when there was a divorce. Why was it that the altar in particular, and not any of the other holy vessels, was used as a metaphor for the tears of divorce? Because the altar is the place where the sacrifices were offered. Hashem is lovingly telling us, "You need to sacrifice for your marriage. But if there's no other choice, I'll be the one to sacrifice."

Hashem is telling us that He personally chose our spouse and would *prefer* that we stay married; but if we are really miserable, then we may get divorced. G-d will put aside His own wishes just to make us happy. If that's not the definition of a good marriage, I don't know what is.

Hashem created us and He therefore knows that we are finite, fickle and fallible. Sometimes we just cannot get along. In a bad marriage both partners become despondent and downhearted and can find no way out. But Hashem, in His infinite kindness, has already anticipated this possibility and has given us a gift called a Get, a Halachic divorce. There is no Mitzvah in suffering as long as we have made every effort to repair the relationship.

When married men and women say that they are in an abusive relationship, I tell them it's impossible; that it's an oxymoron. If there is abuse, then by definition, it is *not* a relationship. When there is real physical or emotional abuse you cannot put up with it, you run for help. Years ago, the Rebbe urged all of us to choose a Mashpia, a mentor to whom we can turn for advice. Having a mentor helps us to avoid bad behaviors, because when we ask for help, we will have to reveal them.

Let's face it, we all know when we are behaving badly. Deep down we know when we are part of the problem and not of the solution, especially when it comes to marriage. G-d chose our Bashert for us and He wants us to make this person happy. Are we doing that? Can we nullify our will for someone else, just as Hashem does for us? This is not to suggest that we become a doormat in the process. We can find creative, loving and, most of all, respectful ways to sweeten our spouses to our way of thinking.

For example, a dear friend of mine was struggling with her husband's reluctance to join her in her journey to becoming completely Shomer Shabbat. He was willing to turn off the TVs around the house before Shabbat, but he insisted that one TV stay on in their bedroom. This was a bone of contention between them that needed to be solved.

"My husband is a businessman," my friend said. "He totally understands deal making. So one day I tried a little negotiation. I said, 'Let's try to have it off for only one month. After that, if you can't live with it, I promise not to mention it again.'" Her husband thought about it and agreed. "That first Shabbat I set the table beautifully," she said "and I made all the foods that he likes for our Shabbat dinner. I got a little nervous when his usual television time began, but my husband is a man of his word and the television stayed off, although he twisted and turned all night."

At the end of the month, to my friend's utter surprise and delight, he agreed to leave it off permanently. He enjoyed the feeling that for one day a week, he was insulated from the outside world. Everything changed for the couple after that. They had learned the art of give and take. When there is reciprocal *respect*, there will be reciprocal *love* and we must do everything in our power to ignite that love.

Marriage should be more give than take. Marriage is not 50-50, it is 200-200. We do our own hundred and also our spouse's hundred. Husband and wife each do whatever it takes to keep the marriage alive.

The Money in the Gemara

The following story took place more than a hundred years ago in a small European Shtetl. It was a time before people used banks to safeguard their money and instead they would bring it to the home of a saintly rabbi or community leader. The rabbi would guarantee the return of the money, but would also use the funds to give free loans to the poor.

One day the door opens in the home of the holy rabbi and Yossel the shoemaker comes in and says, "I have come to repay the money I borrowed from you." He lays the money down on the table in front of the rabbi and leaves.

The rabbi, who is intently engrossed in his learning, tucks the money into the pages of his Gemara and continues his studies, intending to post the transaction as soon as he was done. However, when he finishes learning, he closes the Sefer, puts it back in its accustomed place in the bookshelf and completely forgets about the money lying within.

Some time goes by and the poor of the community come as usual for free loans, but the rabbi realizes something is wrong. He does not have enough money to lend out. He goes back to his books and searches his accounts and finds that Yossel has surprisingly not repaid his loan. Thinking that there must be an unusual situation, he pays Yossel a visit and asks if it's possible that he could return at least part of the money now.

"What do you mean?" says the confused man. "I repaid that loan months ago, even ahead of time." But the rabbi is sure he was not repaid.

Unfortunately, as so often happens, the gossipmongers have a field day and accuse Yossel of trying to steal communal funds. The poor man is ostracized, loses all of his customers and he and his wife and children are reduced to abject poverty.

A full year goes by in these terrible circumstances and one day the rabbi opens the same Gemara he was learning that day and finds the money, just as Yossel had said. He is beside himself and runs straight to Yossel's home, but finds he has moved and is now living in a ramshackle hut. "Please forgive me," he cries. "I made a terrible mistake, I am going to announce on Shabbos to the whole community that you are right and I was wrong."

"I forgive you completely," says Yossel, "but the community is another story. They will think you are only trying to protect me." This is true of human nature; the facts don't always disabuse people of their preconceived notions.

The rabbi thought and thought about what he could do and came up with a novel idea. "Yossel, you have a daughter of marriageable age and I have a son. We will make a Shidduch and invite the whole Shtetl to the wedding."

And so it was, the daughter of the simple shoemaker married the son of the holy rabbi and Yossel was restored to his honorable role in the community.

Hashem makes Shiduchim in so many ways; some obvious, some obscure. Perhaps in this case, Yossel and his family suffered a year of degradation because it was the only path towards connecting these two Bashert souls.

The Splitting of the Sea and Shidduchim

Making a Shidduch is not easy, even G-d agrees it's hard work. How do we know? The Talmud tells us that "making Shidduchim is as difficult for Hashem as Krias Yam Suf." What's the connection between the two?

There is an enigmatic Midrash that when Hashem created the oceans, He told the Yam Suf, the Red Sea, that there would come a time in the future when it would have to go against its very nature. It would be required to split in two so that Hashem's holy children would be able to walk through it. The sea agreed to G-d's request.

But what happened when the B'nai Yisrael finally came to the sea's edge? Nothing at all happened until a man named Nachshon Ben Aminadav bravely walked into the water up to his nostrils. Only then did the sea split. Why the hesitation? The problem was that the sea did not recognize the fledgling Jewish nation. The sea was expecting holiness and piety and instead was faced with a rag-tag band of former slaves, who had sunk to the lowest levels of impurity during their years in Egypt. These could *not* be the holy children whom Hashem had meant.

But then along came Nachshon. His self-sacrifice, his willingness to die Al Kiddush Hashem changed everything. The sea recognized that indeed these are Hashem's special children and it immediately split into two and the B'nai Yisrael walked through on dry land.

The Midrash goes on to say that incredibly, the same thing is true of Shidduchim! Forty days before conception when the names of their prospective spouses are called out in heaven, both Neshamot, both souls, are still in their pristine and innocent state and they cling to each other happily. But then twenty or so years later when they meet on earth, they sometimes don't recognize each other. The intervening years may have sullied their souls to the extent that they are no longer familiar.

That is why it's important when meeting a prospective shidduch to peer through the dusty outer layer and trappings and try to recognize the original diamond shining inside.

Do You Want to Marry Me?

Rabbi Manis Friedman famously says that on your very first date you should ask the following question. Are you interested in marrying *me*? If the answer is yes then you can begin to get to know each other.

Rabbi Friedman is advising that one should not waste time going out with someone who has no intention of getting married right now. Perhaps ever! One woman I know told me that she wasted seven years of her life going out with a man she thought would eventually marry her. He didn't. The saddest part is that those wasted years were not a big deal for *him*. But for a woman who wants children, seven years can be devastating. If you want to get married, don't go out in order to date. Date to determine whether this person is a prospective *marriage* partner.

The second most important question to ask yourself on a date is: Will we respect each other? Respect is a deal-breaking, crucial component in a marriage.

I will never forget meeting a very famous rabbi who would come to Italy from time to time to speak. He was like a king to most of us. Not only was he an amazing scholar and speaker, he was also tall, good-looking and charismatic. On one occasion, his wife accompanied him to the program and I happened to be in the room when she first walked in. I can still see the expression on her husband's face when he saw her approaching. He was so happy to see her; he turned a bright, blushing red. The way he looked at her with so much pride and love, it was as if all of us in the room did not exist.

I had always assumed that his wife would be gorgeous and glamorous. It turns out she was at least a foot shorter than he was, and looked twice his age. But of course, she was beautiful *to him*. It was clear to all of us that this was a woman he deeply respected and that's when I first realized that respect brings love, but love does not always bring respect.

Passion Is for the Movies: True or False?

If you answered true, you are wrong. But you are not alone. I am certain that if we took a survey of young people who are about to get married, they would say that what is depicted in the media is not meant for a couple who want to scrupulously adhere to the laws of Taharat Hamishpacha. And they would be wrong too.

Contrary to what you might have learned, passion is not only halachically permitted, it is essential to marital intimacy. When a couple is in the dating process, *falling in lust* is a prerequisite to falling in love. I can hear you saying, "That's not holy, that's just another message we get from the movies." You are right, but only half right. It is a value that the secular media promotes relentlessly and reprehensibly, but it is also a traditional Jewish ideal. Let me illustrate with the following true story.

A Shliach in Florida told me that his daughter had been dating a young man from a wonderful family, a Talmid Chochom and a real mentsch. He was hoping that this would be her Bashert.

However, after a few dates, his daughter said that the young man was indeed a good person, but she just wasn't feeling any chemistry between them. The Shliach wrote a letter to the Rebbe asking what should be done in this case. The Rebbe's answer was crystal clear. "If there is no chemistry, if there is no physical attraction, do *not* do the Shidduch."

Chemistry is a major ingredient in any marriage. It is not the only one by any means, but it would be foolhardy to ignore those early warning signals. "Lust" is a coarse word that we don't like to use in refined conversation, so we substitute the word "chemistry," but it's one and the same. And without it there can be no Shidduch.

Just listen to what the Ramban writes about intimacy. He says that when a union between husband and wife takes place without passion and desire, the Shechina will not be a partner in that encounter.

Amazing stuff and totally not what we expected, is it? However, the above does not condone acting in a flagrantly immodest manner. The Shulchan Aruch, the Code of Jewish Law, says that everything is permitted between a husband and wife; but that doesn't mean that we need to *do* everything. Obviously this is a very personal decision and should be made with the utmost concern for Tzniut and Kedusha.

Persians have a saying "to open one's face." It is not necessary to open your face, to expose yourself unnecessarily. Modesty does not mean that a woman must hide herself, but she must be aware that she has enormous potential to use her womanhood in a wise way, for a higher spiritual purpose.

The Ramban also teaches us that when a couple is intimate, when they are about to possibly create a new soul, they cannot be in a state of anger, mindlessness or drunkenness. They must be cognizant of the enormous potential this union has to create a soul either in holiness or, G-d forbid, in degradation. There are numerous studies that suggest that even what the parents are *thinking* during conception can influence their unborn child.

When Hashem created the animals, He created them separately as male and female. Man, however, was created both male and female. Adam was first fashioned by G-d with one side male and one side female, and then G-d disconnected them from each other in order to teach us about relationships. To teach us that husband and wife are two halves of one whole. It is only after the Chupah that we become one again.

Hashem did not separate us from the head so that one would be dominant and not from the feet, so that one would be subservient. Hashem separated us from the rib - from the side - so that male and female are equal partners in a G-dly marriage.

Check, Check and Check Again

There is another common dating misconception I would like to address. A Shadchan will tell you it doesn't matter who the prospective in-laws are, it's only the man or woman you're marrying that counts. That's just not true. I have a source for this as well, so you will know I am not making these things up.

Forty days before conception, there is a Bat Kol, a Heavenly voice that announces "This girl, the daughter of so and so, will marry this boy, the son of so and so." Why are the names of the parents included in this prophecy? Because whether we like it or not, we are what our parents taught us to be. We were raised by them and will forever be influenced by what we experienced in their home.

This is a general statement that obviously has exceptions. For example, the family you are considering is known to be good and kind, but they have issues such as divorce, illness or level of observance. Does this mean you automatically say no to the Shidduch? Obviously not. Every family is unique and must be evaluated on their merits, not on their (perhaps irrelevant) issues.

For example, I know a wonderful, highly acclaimed rabbi, whose beautiful first-born daughter married into a family where the parents were of modest means and who were simple, unlearned people. The young lady's parents looked beyond the superficial and saw the sterling character of the prospective family and the Shidduch was made.

When there is a potential Shidduch in the making, ask yourself the following questions. Does he honor his parents? Does she speak disparagingly about her mother, or does he disrespect his father? These are indications that we may not want to go there. Children mirror what they see. While dating, it is important to ask personal and specific questions. Is he stingy with money and affection? Does she have an anger problem? Will he be a good father to our children? Will she maintain the kind of home that I'm looking for?

Many men, regrettably, look only at dress size and too many women look at wallet size. Although these may be concerns, they are hardly the stuff of marriage. Ask the really important questions and remember that all the information you need should be obtained well before there is any emotional involvement because then it is sometimes too hard and too late to let go.

Another good tip to remember is that people on a date can pretend to be someone they are not, but their friends will know the truth, so check out the people they associate with and ask your questions. Ironically, if there is a really deep, dark secret, people will know about it; but the everyday stuff can be just as important. It helps to remember that people do change and evolve and because someone knew them years ago, their report is not necessarily true today.

Speaking evil about someone is a serious sin with disastrous personal and spiritual consequences. There are two occasions, however, where we are permitted and even encouraged, to speak Lashon Hara: in Shidduchim and in business. In both cases the questions we ask can have critical and life-altering consequences and we need truthful answers to our queries, if asked. So the bottom line is, check and recheck and then go with your instinct.

Important Message for Singles

To all of you still-single women and men who have not yet met their Bashert, I want to say something very important. Enjoy your life now. Remember that what you can do now and where you can go now will not always be possible after marriage. Take the time to pursue whatever it is that you want to accomplish in your personal life. Live fully every day and don't play the waiting game. Your life is *not* on hold; it is amazing and thriving and you are living it to the hilt.

When a suitable Shidduch comes along, of course you will pursue it, but it's not going to be the only focus of your days and nights. You have a life - and it's a good one. Married, divorced or still single, you are exactly where Hashem wants you to be right now.

Stories about

Marriage

Be Careful What You Wish For

I asked for strength and...
Hashem gave me difficulties to make me strong
I asked for wisdom and...
Hashem gave me problems to solve
I asked for prosperity and...
Hashem gave me brain and brawn to work
I asked for courage and...
Hashem gave me danger to overcome
I asked for love and...
Hashem gave me troubled people to help
I asked for favor and...
Hashem gave me opportunities
I got nothing that I wanted, but
I received everything I *needed*

One of my very favorite truisms is: "More tears are shed over *answered* prayers than on unanswered ones."

Another very good one is: "May you always get what you want and want what you get." Let's face it; do we really know what we want? Do we really know what's good for us? We may think we do but life has a way of showing us otherwise. That's why when we Daven we should pray to Hashem to give us what we need, which is not necessarily what we want.

On a recent speaking engagement in Brooklyn, I was told that the audience was very erudite, educated and discerning and they would be concerned about whether I practice what I preach. This was rather intimidating and I prayed to Hashem to please put words in my mouth that would penetrate the hearts of my audience. I walked up to the podium and started by asking the women a question. "Ladies, if I told you that I could somehow grant you one wish and one only, what would it be?"

There were various answers: One woman wanted better health, another wanted her child to be a mentsch and *everyone* wanted more Parnassah. But I was holding out for one particular request and finally I got it. A rather sad-looking woman said she wished for better Shalom Bayit.

"Aha," I said. "Your wish has incorporated everybody else's wishes. Because when you have Shalom Bayit, marital harmony, you have everything."

The Mishnah states that Hashem did not find a better blessing for His children than Shalom, peace. Shalom also comes from the Hebrew root Shalem which means complete. If you have Shalom Bayit you have a complete home. When there is peace in the home women can be themselves with confidence and pride. (Little known fact: The word Shalom is also one of the names of G-d and one should therefore not say Shalom in the bathroom.)

I told my audience that I often speak to students on college campuses and I find that invariably many of the boys and girls will tell me that they are not *ever* going to get married. When I ask why the answer is inevitably the same. "Because I remember my parents were always fighting with each other." They have tragically been turned off to the institution of marriage. This is doubly sad because it's so easily preventable. We can have a positive affect on our children's view of marriage if only we would follow one simple rule: never fight in front of them.

Of course every husband and wife will have disagreements - that's normal. It's how we *respond* to them and how we work them out that will make all the difference in the world. In other words, how we fight is crucial to the well-being of our marriage. There are couples that get married with a fairy tale ideal of happily-ever-after. They have the mistaken notion that *they* will be different; that they will never fight or have to work hard on keeping their marriage together, that it will be all hearts and roses because "we are so much in love." I hate to admit it, but I was once one of those people.

It turned out that my husband and I had to overcome so many obstacles during those early years - when I was farther ahead in my Yiddishkeit than he was. I wanted us to do everything quickly and simultaneously, and he wanted to take it gradually.

For example, I wanted to cover my hair and my husband adamantly and vocally disagreed. In my naiveté, I hastily wrote a self-righteous letter to the Rebbe saying that I want to do the "correct" thing but my husband doesn't want me to. So shouldn't I just do it anyway?

I was so certain the Rebbe would say that I was absolutely right, but I couldn't have been more wrong. First and foremost the Rebbe told me, "Do not fight about religion." The Rebbe told me not to do anything unless and until my husband was in total agreement.

I understood from the Rebbe's answer that my husband must have felt that I was abandoning him, that I was choosing G-d over him. This was not the effect I was hoping for; it was only turning him against Hashem.

There was another thing I used to do that I finally realized was counterproductive. I would tell my husband, "You don't really love me because if you did, you would do this for me." Ladies, please don't make the same mistake I did. Never tell your spouses that they don't love you. You don't want them to think that maybe you're *right*. You don't want to put the thought into their heads that, "Hey, my wife knows me very well and if *she* thinks I don't love her, maybe I really don't."

So I learned the hard way to turn the situation around. I started to say, "What would you do without me? You know you're crazy about me, you know you love me so much." My positive words changed our situation into a constructive one.

My second piece of advice from the Rebbe was to get someone else to influence my husband, someone whom he trusts and respects. Whew! What a relief that was. The Rebbe was telling me in so many words that I didn't marry my husband to become his rabbi. I married him to become his wife.

My husband Benjamin with our grandson Rephael Gemal.

I also realized that every time I would say to my husband, "Do this, don't do that," I was also subtly giving him the message that our marriage was a hassle and that I was no longer any fun to be with. When I stopped giving him instructions, our marriage almost immediately improved. Now I aspire to be as spiritual as *my husband* is.

Thank G-d my prayers were answered and Hashem gave me what I needed and not what (I thought) I wanted.

Marriage Is What You Make of It

It has been proven that when a couple interacts lovingly first thing in the morning and last thing in the evening, the hours in between will be just fine. (You're welcome!)

I must begin this topic with a caveat. Yes, marriage is what you and your spouse make of it; but this applies to two relatively normal people. If either the husband or wife has serious emotional issues, professional help is required. You *cannot* do this by yourselves and your efforts will only lead to futility and frustration.

Most of us are not, thank G-d, in that category; we are simply human beings with different backgrounds, skills and emotions. The trick is to blend and merge all the characteristics that make each of us uniquely who we are, without losing our own identities in the process.

Shoes and Sensitivity

We all remember the story of the burning bush. When Moshe came closer to check it out, Hashem stopped him and said, "Remove your shoes from your feet because you are standing on holy ground."

What difference did it make whether Moshe was wearing shoes or not? Are bare feet more appropriate on holy ground than shoes? Not necessarily, but G-d was teaching Moshe a lesson about relationships and about sensitivity.

Although shoes are quite the fashion statement these days, that was not their original purpose. Shoes were worn in order to form a barrier between our feet and the ground, to keep us safe from the heat and the stones of the pavement and allow us to walk securely. Conversely, if we took our shoes off, we would tread gingerly - we would be sensitive to every imperfection in the street, to every tiny pebble on our path.

Moshe would soon be the leader of the Jewish people and Hashem wanted him to be extra sensitive to their pain; hence he was told to remove his shoes.

I am here to tell you that marriage is also holy ground, and husbands and wives must metaphorically remove their shoes as well. We must employ the same sensitivity so that we may feel each other's pain.

There is a well-known story about a certain rabbi who drove his Rebbetzin to a doctor's appointment. When they entered the examination room the rabbi said, "Doctor, my wife's foot is hurting *us*!" Taking her to the doctor was not merely an act of chauffeuring for him - it was so much more because his wife's pain was his pain as well.

"Love and Marriage Go Together Like a Horse and Carriage." Do They?

Hashem told us very explicitly what we should look for in a prospective spouse. Right at the beginning of the Torah, in the book of Genesis, we learn that when Avraham dispatched Eliezer to find a wife for his son Yitzchak, Eliezer prayed to Hashem as follows: "And it will be that the maiden to whom I will say 'lower your pitcher and I will drink' and she will say 'drink and I will also water your camels,' her have You designated for Your servant, for Yitzchak."

Eliezer knew that his master wanted him first and foremost to find a woman of good character. Rivkah met that qualification superbly and also exhibited the trait of humility. She covered her face when she saw Yitzchak coming from afar; she nullified herself for him because she recognized that he had a very lofty soul. Conversely, Rivkah exhibited true inner strength and wisdom when she arranged for her son, Yaakov, to get the blessings from his father, because she knew intuitively that he was the rightful heir.

The Torah then tells us something very important about love and marriage. Unlike the famous old song, it does not necessarily follow in that order. It tells us that Yitzchak married Rivkah and only *afterwards* does it say that he loved her. Love is a work in progress and it has no end date.

Rabbi Manis Friedman famously teaches that when a couple is dating they should never think to themselves that "he has potential" or "she could be the right one with a few changes."

Rabbi Friedman says that when you're dating you should never look for potential. You should be totally comfortable with who the person is at that moment. After marriage however, you should *always* consider your spouse as a work in progress, as having untapped potential to be the best husband or wife ever. In a marriage, you always compromise.

What's So Special About the Ring Finger?

It's not difficult to have Shalom Bayit when we are newlyweds. The excitement of the new relationship is overwhelming and we are certain that we will always be as happy as we are now.

As time goes by the luster in the marriage begins to dull just a little and our connection to each other gets familiar rather than fabulous. Husband and wife can begin to drift apart when they see the raw emotions exhibited by couples in movies and novels, and think, "What happened to us?" If this sounds like *your* marriage, allow me to share something that can help alleviate these feelings.

Let's focus on the Chupah ceremony; that glorious moment when bride and groom are standing under the canopy and the groom places the ring on the index finger of the bride. The ring remains there until the Chupah is over and only then does the bride remove it and place it on her ring finger. What does all this mean and what can we learn from this?

There is a vein in the index finger that goes directly to the heart. When a doctor or nurse places a sensor on our index finger during a checkup, it's to measure how much oxygen our heart is supplying. The index finger is attached to the heart, to the emotions. Under the Chupah, our hearts must be as one; our deep love and strong emotions should be palpable.

Once we are married, however, the relationship should evolve into the ring finger. Why? Because the ring finger is the most gentle and non-aggressive one on our hands. That's one reason makeup artists advise us to apply eye cream with the ring finger only, to avoid pulling the sensitive eye tissue.

When we first get married, we do so with the passion and desire needed for us to dedicate ourselves fully to our spouse. But to sustain that marriage, we have to employ the most delicate and refined conduct and have a relationship that is based on respect, kindness and sensitivity. Let's not learn about marriage from Hollywood; let's learn it from our traditional Jewish marriage customs.

The Hunchback in the Mirror

What happens when despite our best efforts, our spouses just don't live up to our expectations? Perhaps she is not the greatest homemaker or mother and he is not the highest earner or most learned scholar. Did we marry the wrong person?

If we truly believe that marriages are Bashert then we have to say, of course not. Hashem does not make mistakes when He pairs up a man and a woman. It is *we* who get blinded by our own shortcomings. The Baal Shem Tov taught that when we perceive a fault in someone, it means that we ourselves have that same fault, but we don't see it.

In times gone by, a matchmaker would seek out a woman of good character and a man of Torah scholarship and a marriage was arranged. Often, the prospective bride and groom did not meet until just before the Chupah. Sometimes, they didn't like what they saw.

In the following story, which is attributed to the Divrei Chaim, his bride took one look at her intended bridegroom and realized she had been lied to. He was lame and hunchbacked, while she was young and beautiful. The rabbi was called, but even he could not convince the reluctant bride to go ahead with the Shidduch.

The bridegroom pleaded with the young woman to give him five minutes. She agreed and they went into a room which was dominated by a large mirror. The prospective bridegroom limped slowly forward and stood in front of the mirror and asked the young woman to stand next to him. When she looked into the mirror at the two of them, she saw that instead of a maimed hunchback staring back at her, the mirror reflected a strong, healthy and handsome man standing at her side. To her utter astonishmenent, she was now the one who was lame and hunchbacked.

The Divrei Chaim gently explained to his bride that in heaven it had been Bashert that *she* would be the one with the deformities. "Out of my love for you, I begged Hashem to reverse this and give *me* the hunchback and He listened to my plea." The young woman was so moved, she agreed to the marriage and they had many good years together and were blessed with healthy children.

When Hashem created Chava, the Torah says that He put Adam to sleep and then removed a rib. Why was it necessary for us to know that Adam was asleep? Because Hashem is trying to tell us that when we see a fault in our spouse, we should close our eyes and *pretend* to be asleep. We should not peer too closely at their deficiencies but search more wisely for their unique virtues.

Persian Betrothals

I come from a Mashhadi Persian community (although I have never been to Iran). This close knit, extremely traditional and low-profile community is known for marrying amongst its own.

This practice began many generations ago during a pogrom in Mashhad, Iran, when the Moslems threatened to kill the Jews if they did not convert to Islam. Like the Marranos before them, the Mashhadi Jews pretended to convert but lived as secret Jews and continued to observe their Yiddishkeit scrupulously in private.

Here I am giving a talk to a group of Persian women.

One of the solutions they found to ensure that their children would never marry a Moslem was to betroth them at a very young age - sometimes even at birth. Thus if anyone not from their community would ask for a girl's hand in marriage, they could truthfully answer that the girl was already betrothed.

These marriages, although predestined, were sometimes obviously mismatched. Their personalities clashed, there were character faults or they just never learned to love each other. But what is most impressive about the statistics in this community is that there was absolutely no divorce! (In recent years, in the United States, there have been some isolated cases of divorce.)

For the good people of Mashhad, there were no questions about whether their marriage was successful, no doubting whether their mates were suitable. One just accepted, as a fact of life, that their spouse was Bashert and that they would remain married for life. (Think Tevya and Golda.) When we accept without question that our spouse is ours for life, then there is no room for anything *but* Shalom Bayit.

I believe that every one of these women was a true Aishet Chayil because they kept their homes together in the midst of great adversity. Their Mikvah was a river, frozen in the winter. They would bake Matzah in secret and their level of Tzniut, their absolute modesty, was something straight from our Matriarchs. They accepted their lot in life and created beautiful Jewish homes and generations of Jewish offspring.

The Rebbe's Marriage Advice

I had the unbelievable Zchut of personally getting advice from the Rebbe on many occasions. Very often the advice was also for the married couples that I was counseling. The Rebbe always stressed that observing the laws of Taharat Hamishpacha strictly and meticulously, was imperative in achieving Shalom Bayit. I have already cited many cases where the Rebbe's sage advice was taken and how it achieved incredible results. Here are a few more examples. We can never hear enough.

Dina was on the verge of a nervous breakdown! She was suffering in a marriage that had gone totally sour. Her husband was cold and distant, her health had deteriorated and she got through her days only with the help of anti-depressants.

When she asked my advice, I suggested that she come with me to the Rebbe for dollars. The Rebbe told her that her situation would improve if she kept Taharat Hamishpacha. At that, she laughed bitterly, "What's the point of going to the Mikvah? My husband is like a stranger to me."

I knew that the Rebbe had already told her not to get divorced, so I insisted that she fulfill *her* responsibility in the marriage and I personally took her to the Mikvah. A melancholy, depressed and sad woman went into the waters that night and an entirely different person emerged. I will always remember the glow on Dina's face as she stepped out of the Mikvah. Her eyes were sparkling and she was actually smiling, something she had not done in a long, long time. She told me that when she was in the Mikvah, she felt all her previous tension fade away. The next morning she called to say that for the first time in months she did not need any medication to fall asleep.

The best part of this story of course is that the couple did not get divorced, are still married and they even had a new baby daughter.

Susan was a recent Baalat Teshuva who was on an upward path in her spirituality. Susan was delighted that her husband was joining her on this journey and he had already agreed to keep the basics: Shabbat, Taharat Hamishpacha and Kashrut. Her husband, however, was very emphatic about not going any further than that and he forbade her to cover her hair or do any other "unnecessary" Mitzvot. She had written to the Rebbe who advised patience and told her to maintain their Shalom Bayit, to keep the peace at all costs. Susan tried to follow this advice and it worked for a while. But she was remained unhappy about her level of observance and really wanted to do more.

When some of her friends, and even a few rabbis, advised her to start doing more Mitzvot regardless of her husband's objections, she decided to listen. But first she wrote to the Rebbe and told him about her decision to start observing more stringently. She was certain that the Rebbe

I was blessed to receive dollars from the Rebbe on many occasions.

would be encouraging and she asked him only for a Bracha. Susan was used to receiving answers from the Rebbe almost immediately, but this time it took a few days. When the answer did come, it was unexpected and surprising. The Rebbe wrote, "And what will you tell your husband when he asks you the *reason* for the changes you are making?"

The Rebbe was concerned for the couple's Shalom Bayit above all, demonstrating once again his concern and sensitivity for the holy institution of marriage.

Disposable Society, Disposable Spouses

Would it shock you to learn that in Tel Aviv, two out of three marriages end in divorce? You're probably thinking that in secular Tel Aviv I may be right, but in our Frum communities? In Jerusalem, Borough Park, Monsey, etc., it will never happen.

Think again. Statistics show that never before in the history of the world has divorce been so prevalent in our Jewish world. This is so devastating that I need to repeat it. Never before have there been as many divorces in our communities as there are today.

How did we get to this appalling place? There is a plethora of reasons, but one of them stands out from the rest. It can be summed up in one word, disposable. Think paper plates, cutlery, water bottles, diapers, wipes, Swiffers, the list goes on. Everything is disposable; everything can be replenished and replaced by a brand-new, shinier version. Tragically, this trend has trickled down to include husbands and wives.

There is a solution to this deplorable state of affairs and it's called Shalom Bayit. Nothing is more important or more tantalizing in our world today than peace. We all want a peaceful world, but peace must begin in our homes; we must give the goal of marital harmony the full respect it deserves. It's always been a mystery to me that we run to psychologists, to parenting seminars, to Shidduchim forums, to weight reduction clinics, etc. But a class on Shalom Bayit? We are too embarrassed because people might think our marriages need improvement. Duh!

The well known story of the Isha Sotah, the woman who has aroused the suspicions of her husband, can teach us a lesson about just how precious marriage is to Hashem and to what lengths we must go to save it.

During the days of the Beit Hamikdash, if a woman was suspected by her husband of infidelity, the Kohen Gadol was instructed to bring the couple to the Temple, where he took a piece of parchment and wrote two verses from the Torah on it, containing G-d's ineffable name. Then he dipped the parchment in water, thereby erasing the name of Hashem. Ordinarily it is a sin to erase the holy Name but G-d said, "In order to make peace between husband and wife, you may even erase my name. Nothing is more important."

The Rebbe once said that if Hashem was willing to sacrifice Himself in order to restore peace between husband and wife, who are we to do less? It does not have to be my way or the highway, and we can suppress our egos for a higher cause. And as Hashem Himself taught us, there is no greater cause than our own marriage.

Fire And Ice

I once asked my husband if he would have preferred to be married to someone a little calmer than I am, someone more like he is. His answer? "Absolutely not. I would be bored to tears."

One of the ten plagues that rained down on the Egyptians was the plague of hailstones. Rashi comments that the hailstones were a combination of fire and ice and the only way they could possibly co-exist was because G-d told them to. The same goes for many marriages. One of the partners may be as cold as ice and the other as passionate as fire - the Mars/Venus syndrome. Can they be happy together?

We have to remember that Hashem created *both* planets and there is no right or wrong one. Two opposites can actually create a balanced marriage. Two clones, as my husband so aptly said, would be "boring."

Communication Tips From the Ten Commandments

I once heard a wise woman say, "Let your husband win the argument because if he loses, what does that say about you? It says that you are married to a loser."

Don't get me wrong. I am not advocating becoming a Shmatte, a rag or a doormat, and giving in indiscriminately to every argument. That road only leads to resentment, frustration and even further arguments ahead.

We have to keep our eyes on our ultimate goal of Shalom Bayit. That ideal is simply to have *no* fighting or ill feelings towards your spouse. We can achieve that by having respect for our spouses or *giving* respect even when we don't feel it.

When G-d gave us the Ten Commandments, He chose His location carefully. Hashem picked a desolate desert and silenced all of creation so there would be no distractions. Hashem told us three days in advance that He had something to say to us, so that we could be properly prepared. G-d also chose His words carefully and distilled the entire Torah into only 10 utterances.

When we have something important to say to our spouses, we too, should be particular about when and where to voice those feelings. If he is hungry, tired and had a hard day at work, we might as well save our breath; he will not be receptive to a single word we say. Conversely, when she is in the midst of dealing with a new baby, a cranky toddler and two kids who need help with their homework, absolutely anything he says will surely backfire.

Why do we think it's necessary to blurt out our issues the moment they enter our thoughts? We need to calm down, count to one hundred and then see if the confrontation can't wait another few hours. By that time it usually turns into a non-issue altogether.

Get Your Own Tea – Or Not

My good friend Malkah always believed that it was a given in life that children learn from their parents. During a recent visit to her children's home, she found the tables had turned and she was learning from *them*.

She told me that her daughter is a busy wife and mom and like most young women she is always juggling her myriad responsibilities. That evening her daughter was rushing around trying to make dinner, cleaning up the clutter and keeping an eye on her little ones – all at the same time. Even with her help it was a hectic few hours.

In the midst of this turmoil, her husband asked his wife to please make him a cup of tea. Her daughter didn't answer him and continued her rushing around. After about ten minutes had passed without any tea, he again asked if he could have a cup. She turned around to him and with a beautiful smile said, "What, you finished the first one already?" And they both burst out laughing.

"I was so amazed," said Malkah. "Instead of saying 'don't you see how busy I am' or 'get your own tea' my daughter made a conscious decision to avoid what would surely turn into an argument. She chose to use gentle humor instead and it worked."

Humor is an excellent tool and, used effectively, will diffuse many potential confrontations. Of course it cannot poke fun or be unkind to the other person; it must be used lovingly to achieve the desired effect. The bottom line is: Don't take yourself so seriously. Learn how to laugh at situations that will not matter an hour from now.

In all situations, first ask yourself: "Will I care about this in a month, in a year, in five years?" Then act accordingly.

My friend's story with the tea reminds me of a story about the Rebbe and his doctor. During a routine exam, the Rebbe noticed that the doctor seemed unusually busy and harried. When he was done, the doctor suggested to the Rebbe that he was working too hard and should slow down, the Rebbe said that he does relax because his daily schedule includes sitting down and having a cup of tea with his Rebbetzin, for at least fifteen minutes every day.

Then the Rebbe reversed the doctor/patient relationship and said: "*You* should try to do the same."

In today's technological and overly scheduled environment, time has become more precious than money. Time is crucial in marriage and we need to create a space for our spouses. That time needs to be carefully planned and scheduled; it never just happens.

A young couple I was counseling wanted to know whether I had a top ten list for achieving Shalom Bayit. I told them that a sense of humor and making time for our spouse are definitely at the top.

Are You a Willow or an Oak?

The trait of flexibility would also make it to my top ten list for marriage. Being flexible is one of the benefits of marrying at a young age; the couple is not yet set in their ways.

The Rebbe once said something beautiful on flexibility. He asked a rhetorical question: Imagine that there is an oak tree and a willow tree planted next to each other. A sudden hurricane storms through the field. Which tree will withstand the mighty winds? Certainly not the oak tree; it stands too firm, too inflexible to the buffeting winds. It is the gently swaying willow that would still be standing when the storm had subsided.

So be like the willow tree, allow yourself to bend, give in and be flexible whenever possible. The only exception to this rule is in the area of Halacha. If there are spiritual ramifications to an argument, a competent Rav should be consulted.

Sometimes a couple will tell me that no matter what they do, it's no use. "We just bring out the worst in each other, we just keep on fighting." In a letter that the Rebbe once wrote to a couple, he advised them, "When your partner is throwing bullets at you, throw flowers."

In other words, you cannot fight with someone who just refuses to fight. This doesn't mean that you always have to give in; it simply means to convey the message that 'I don't want to fight with you.' It is a delicate yet amazingly strong position; don't rise to the argument, let it go. I have a theory that two people cannot be angry at each other *at the same time.* Take turns.

Even a Bad Marriage Is Bashert

Husbands and wives will sometimes tell me, "If I had only realized how mean she was or how stingy he is, we would never have gotten married."

We are married to the person whom we are *supposed to be* married to at that time. Hashem does not make mistakes. In fact, G-d blinded us so that we would *not see* those character flaws when we first met. This is proof that the marriage was Bashert, pre-destined. Even a bad marriage is Bashert for reasons known only to our Creator and that's why we have halachically acceptable divorce, because not every marriage can be saved,

Nonetheless, when we internalize the concept that the person we are married to is meant for us and is *not* a mistake, it makes it that much easier to try and work through our issues before they become insurmountable. Don't put yourself in the mindset where you have one foot out the door at all times.

And finally, we dare not take Shalom Bayit for granted. There is a beautiful suggestion from our rabbis. During the Birchat Kohanim in Shul, when we hear the last word "Shalom," we should have in mind that the peace, the Shalom, must begin first and foremost with our spouse.

Sorry, I Have to Hang Up Now

When women get really busy and try hard to live up to the superwoman ideal, something will inevitably fall by the wayside. In my counseling experience, that something is very often our husband. At the end of the day we are sometimes so tired, even freaking out, that we are only too willing to dump all that stress on our husbands as soon as they walk in the door.

If, by some stroke of good fortune, there is a day when we are not stressed out, then we are on our iPhones or logged into Facebook when our husbands come home. We give them a perfunctory hello and quickly resume our conversations. If this sounds familiar, let's resolve to do better and take a lesson in how to greet a husband from the Rebbe's wife, the Rebbetzin Chaya Mushka.

The Rebbetzin was exemplary in her total dedication to Shalom Bayit. She would wait up for the Rebbe to come home every evening, even though it was often in the wee hours of the night.If she happened to be on the telephone when the Rebbe walked in, she would say to the person on the other end, "I'm sorry, I have to hang up now. I have a guest." She was certainly not afraid that the Rebbe would be upset, but she hung up the phone because he came first. And not because he was the Rebbe, but because he was her husband. Who else should come first?

The Rebbetzin always greeted her husband with a cup of hot tea and the Rebbe would then tell her a lighthearted anecdote or joyful incident that happened that day. Remember that the Rebbe had the weight of the world on his shoulders. He dealt with his Chassidim's personal problems, with serious communal issues and with the world at large; but that's not what he wanted to share with his wife initially. The first thing the Rebbe wanted to share with his Rebbetzin was Simcha.

Once, after a speech to a group of women in California, I received a telephone call from one of the participants. "Mrs. Karmely, you remember telling us about the Rebbe's wife hanging up the phone when her husband came home? Well, this made such an impression on me, I decided to practice it too. When I heard my husband coming in, I *pretended* to be on the phone and said loudly enough for him to hear, 'I have to hang up now, I have a special guest.' I can't begin to tell you what a huge difference this simple act has made in our marriage. I've said it often enough now, that I really mean it, and my husband is so flattered, he feels ten feet tall. It has cemented our relationship."

The Baal Shem Tov said that a Neshama comes down to this world for only one reason: to do a favor for another. That's our soul's entire purpose. Let us all pledge to begin doing that favor first for the people we live with.

An Onion on Marriage

A man once came to his rabbi with a profound question. He wanted to become a better husband but didn't know how. What should he do? The rabbi's answer was a succinct three words. "Emulate an onion." He went on to explain. "When your wife makes a pot of chicken soup, she always adds an onion, although she knows that almost no one in your family will eat it. So why does she put it in? Because the onion gives the rest of the soup a better flavor." The man got the message. The onion is *selfless*, it's happy to be cooked solely to flavor the rest of the broth.

Marriage and life in general is not all about us. It's about what we can do to help the people around us. Marriage is not about me, it's not about you, it's not even about *us*. It's about the bigger picture. It's about our G-d-given purpose to make the world just a little bit holier and to prepare it for the coming of Mashiach. I can't think of a better place to begin this holy task than within our own families. You want to be a better father, a better mother or a better child? Make like an onion!

Thank You Avraham Fried

Avraham Fried, the international Chassidic superstar, is much more than an amazing entertainer and singer. He is a true Chassid of the Rebbe and is beloved by his fans and by his peers in the music business because he is, above all, a real mentsch.

Several years ago, he did a special kindness for my family and I'm not sure I ever thanked him enough. So Avremel, here is my overdue thanks to you... and for my readers, this is the story.

My family and I were in the midst of preparations for a wonderful Simcha; our youngest daughter Daniella Miriam was B"H getting married.

As my husband and I were making up the guest list, I said that I would like to invite Avraham Fried to the wedding. My husband is a fan, but he felt that there was no point in inviting him because "he won't come to the wedding, he's too busy." I felt that if the date didn't conflict with one of his concerts perhaps he would come. "I really doubt it," my husband said, "but I'm willing to try. Furthermore, if Avraham Fried does come to the wedding, I will become a Chassid."

At that time, my husband was - how shall I say it graciously - not enamored of Chassidim and everyone knew it. So I told him to say "B'li Neder." "Don't make a vow that you won't keep." But he assured me that he was making a real vow. "I will wear a black hat, grow a beard and do everything. But don't worry, he's not coming to the wedding."

Of course with that kind of incentive, I definitely sent the invitation. Avremel replied that due to his busy concert schedule, he unfortunately could not attend. Of course my husband triumphantly said, "I told you so."

A few weeks after our daughter's wedding, I ran into the superstar at the wedding of his nephew. "Avremel," I said jokingly, "you know that because of you, my husband is not a Chassid." He looked absolutely stunned. "What did I do?" I told him the whole story and when I

Avraham Fried in our home.

was done, Avremel said, "Listen, I will come to your home right after Shabbos and do a private concert just for the new bride and groom. Buy a few bagels and set it up for me."

Now it was my turn to look stunned. I just couldn't believe he would do this, but he insisted, and said it would make him very happy. I went right out and bought the refreshments for the evening. I still have that receipt. The total was $77.00 exactly. (Any number that has 770 in it is considered a good omen by Chabad Chassidim.)

Motzoei Shabbos came and so did Avremel, accompanied by a musician. My daughter and son-in-law were ecstatic, to say the least; he is their favorite singer, as he is mine. And what a show he put on. He sang, he spoke, and he told stories all imbued with his special warmth and Torah teachings. His voice touches the very Neshama of all who hear him.

But the climax of the evening was yet to come. It was already past midnight when Avremel brought out a large shopping bag. He pulled out a Kapote (the traditional Chassidic long black coat) and a black hat and presented them to my husband. As he put them on, Avremel movingly sang the Shehechiyanu blessing. There was not a dry eye in the house. What a poignant moment that was for all of us.

Our private concert. Left to right: Me, daughter Esther, daughter Daniella Miriam, my husband Benjamin, Avraham, and our son in law Elroyi Beniamin.

This kindness by Avraham Fried did much to break the ice around my husband's heart and helped thaw his "problem" with Chassidim. He was very affected by Avremel's humility and lack of ego as well as by the melodies he sang that night. Today he is a completely Frum Jew, with beautiful Yirat Shomayim. We are so blessed.

Avremel, thank you again and may you go from strength to strength in inspiring all with your amazing G-d-given talents. Yasher Koach!

Top Twelve Tips To Tranquility

Is your spouse caring, thoughtful, super-sensitive and a good provider to boot? If that's so, consider yourself one of the fortunate few and never, *ever* take it for granted.

But if you are like most of us, you probably have one or two (or more) Shalom Bayit issues that you are struggling with. Marital discord and divorce are rampant in our society today. Do you ever wonder why this is so?

I think about it a lot and I know for sure that the reason is a spiritual one. The Rebbe taught that it is specifically at this point in our history, when we are nearing the end of Golus, that the forces of impurity are doubling their efforts to ensure that there is a lack of Shalom Bayit in our homes.

These forces are working overtime to bring hostility and conflict into our marriages, precisely *because* there is nothing more important in the Jewish home than harmony and tranquility. Without Shalom Bayit, we hurt in so many ways. We suffer psychologically, physically and emotionally. Our health is affected and psychosomatic illness ensues. We become angry, bitter and sad and our relationships suffer. The ones we love the most, our families and our friends, are the ones who are forced to bear the brunt of our discord.

The *fruits* of Shalom Bayit on the other hand, are health, happiness, security and self-esteem. When we are united, we can face every adversity with serenity and strength.

Over the years, I have counseled many couples who were seemingly trapped in unhappy and even combative marriages. With the help of Hashem and the Brachot of our beloved Rebbe, I have seen amazing improvements, some of them quite miraculous. It may surprise you that in all these years, the Rebbe never advised even one of those unhappy women to seek a divorce. He always encouraged them to stay married and to try even harder to make it work.

I would like to begin with a few *spiritual* suggestions. I have a relative in Yerushalayim who is a Mekubal, known for his many miraculous deeds and uncanny foresight. The following suggestions are the ones he offers to the many women who come to him for help. These ideas can only come from a holy person because they are holy in nature.

1. Make an effort to regularly Daven Kabbalat Shabbat on Friday nights.
2. Avoid arguments on Shabbat.
3. Check your Ketubah for possible errors.
4. Recite Segulot, prayers, for Shalom Bayit. (If you would like to receive some of these prayers, please contact me.)

The following are some simple and obvious remedies, which can both help a bad marriage and improve a good one.

1. You do not marry the man you love. You love the man you marry.

2. Dress for your husband as attractively as you do for friends or strangers. There is a Midrash that says that when the Manna fell from heaven in the desert, Hashem also rained down eye makeup and perfumes for the women so that they could beautify themselves for their husbands. My mother, of blessed memory, worked hard all day taking care of her home and her six children k"h, but I remember that she always applied fresh lipstick before my father came home from work.

3. The old cliché that the best way to a man's heart is through his stomach, is corny but true. Every man appreciates a wholesome meal and a delicious dessert. It makes them feel that we have thought about them during the day and that we are trying to please them. On the flip side, some husbands take this for granted and sometimes need a gentle reminder that we would like a verbal thank-you for our culinary efforts.

4. Keep your home clean, neat and organized. Organization or seder is a very important component of the home because it allows it to function properly. We women are truly privileged to create a miniature sanctuary in our homes, a Mikdash M'at, in which our families will thrive spiritually and physically. For that to happen, the home must maintain structure, cleanliness and organization; each one in accordance with the strengths and capabilities of the woman who is running it. (Note: It does not have to pass the white glove test.)

5. **Remember this maxim: Women need appreciation and men need respect.** My brother-in-law, Dr. Yosef Dovid Halbfinger, a marriage and guidance counselor, has helped many couples achieve Shalom Bayit. He swears by the above concept.

6. **Make quality time for one another.** This may seem elementary (my dear Watsons) but you would be shocked at how many couples never take the time just to be together. Couples need to go out alone, without their children or friends, at least once a week. As difficult as it seems, and as tired as you are, this is possible and works wonders. It is well worth the hassle, expense and effort of babysitters. Even a walk around the block helps. Make sure to talk only about non-stressful subjects and definitely not about household or work matters.

I once had a choice of where to go on vacation. I wanted to go and visit my parents in Eretz Yisrael, while my husband wanted me to go with him on a trip to Bangkok. I wrote to the Rebbe and asked his advice. The very next day I received an answer: "Go to Bangkok with your husband." This same situation repeated itself for three years, always with the same answer. What good advice this is for everyone. I could go see my parents a different time, without my husband.

7. **Do not postpone the Mikvah night** except in cases of illness or emergency. There is no other good reason to warrant postponing immersion in the Mikvah and we can never underestimate the spiritual significance of going to the Mikvah at the appointed time.

8. **A righteous woman influences her husband's will** in a gentle and feminine manner until it becomes his choice as well. "Isha K'sheira Oseh Retzon Ba'alah." We women have been blessed with Bina Yetaira, an extra measure of intuition that our husbands don't have. Therefore, they truly cannot be blamed for being oblivious to something that seems obvious to us. When we feel we are right, especially in spiritual matters, we need to express our feelings in a loving and gentle manner without badgering, blaming or anger.

9. **The Mitzvah of Ahavat Yisrael, loving your fellow Jew, applies to your husband as well.** If G-d can forgive us so many times and is magnanimous enough not to keep reminding us of our sins, why can't we forgive our husbands? (Without self-righteously reminding them of how great we are.) A brilliant book that is guaranteed to help any marriage is "Doesn't Anyone Blush Anymore?"

by Rabbi Manis Friedman. If you read it years ago, I strongly suggest that you re-read it.

10. Accept the fact that the man you are married to is exactly the one that you were meant to marry. Just as we appreciate without question that our brother is our brother and our father is our father, how can we possibly not realize and accept that our husband was meant to be our husband? We are fulfilling our purpose and mission in life by being married to him, both in good times and in difficult times. We are one Neshama, one entity that was separated in heaven, in order that we would be reunited as husband and wife in this world.

The Baal Shem Tov said that when we see a fault in another person, it is but a reflection of our own faults. Let's not judge our husbands, lest we be found guilty as well. A better way of dealing is: My husband may not be perfect, but he is perfect for me because he is mine.

11. Desperate times call for desperate measures. An old friend once told me about her brother-in-law who had suddenly and tragically passed away in his sleep. "I got goose bumps when I realized that this could happen to anyone at any time." That very day she resolved not to say or do anything to her husband that she might later regret. She began to picture him in a different light - would this be the last time she would ever see him? Is this what she would want her last words or actions to be? Admittedly, this is a gruesome and extreme remedy but desperate times call for desperate measures. When the home situation reaches an unbearable level, this can be the most sobering and effective technique. It might even cause us to say "I'm sorry" first.

12. The Torah is the foundation for a happy home. Make it the basis for your marriage. I once remarked to a friend who is a Baalat Teshuvah and happily remarried, that I was so glad she had finally found contentment after suffering a disastrous first marriage. Her reply was a revelation to me. She said "Sarah, if I had been observant during my first marriage, I would have handled things very differently. I might have never even gotten divorced. I realize now that the Torah is actually the solution for a happy home and my husband and I have made it the heart and core of our marriage. There is no question as to who wins an argument - it's neither me nor my husband - it's only the Torah's teachings."

Two Eyes, Two Ears and Your Mother-In-Law

When Rabbi Yosef Yitzchak Schneerson known as the Frierdiker Rebbe, was about four years old, he asked his father, the Rebbe Rashab: "Why do we have two eyes?" His father explained to him, "We use the left eye to look at candy and other material things and we use the right eye to look at a fellow Jew." Or in another version, his father told him, "We use one eye to see the good in others and the other eye to see the faults in ourselves."

The above is good advice in life, but in a marriage it is priceless. If we are married, it goes without saying that we need to use our right eye and our right eye only, to look at our spouses. G-d chose the *placement* of our eyes carefully; he placed them in the front of our heads. This teaches us not to keep looking back at bygone slights and quarrels, not to drag up past issues especially with our spouses. Of course we have to learn from our mistakes or we are doomed to repeat them. I am referring to the constant rehashing of things that only bring further rancor and bitterness. Once an issue is resolved, leave it in the past. Look ahead.

In One Ear and Out the Other

Hashem also blessed us with two ears so that we may let some things go in one ear and out the other. An example of this is a hurtful comment about an in-law. It happens. Let it go. It's shocking to me how many issues in a marriage are caused by friction between in-laws. Petty jealousies, insecurities and hypersensitivity all build up and can fester and brew endlessly. But it can be overcome by being aware of one simple fact. The Mitzvah to honor our parents also includes honoring our in-laws.

Baruch Hashem I have become a mother-in-law and thank G-d I also *have* a mother-in-law. I see how delicate the balance is. Girls, give your mothers-in-law a break. One day you too shall have a daughter-in-law and then you will realize how difficult that role is. Mothers-in-law cannot do anything right. If we try to help out, we are being nosy; if we don't help, we are being selfish.

I have a wonderful daughter-in-law, Chana Devorah, G-d bless her. She is an exemplary wife and mother and hopefully her children will see how she treats me and act accordingly when they get married.

There is an old Persian saying, "The sign of a good mother-in-law is a bleeding palm and a bleeding tongue." When you so badly want to give *unsolicited* advice and opinions, dig your nails into your palms until they bleed, and bite your tongue at the same time. I try to give advice only when I'm asked and I don't offer my opinions too often either. That way, I do occasionally get asked, "What do you think?" By the way, there are only two things you should give a son-in-law: Money and respect.

Listening Without Hearing

The Rebbe's wife, Rebbetzin Chaya Mushka, once had a visitor in her home and he received a phone call while he was there. He asked permission to answer it and after a few moments he hung up. He said to the Rebbetzin, "You probably heard the conversation." She answered, "No, I didn't hear it. My father taught me that in certain situations it's possible to be listening without hearing."

This is good advice for maintaining another's privacy, but it's a bad technique in a marriage. All too often, we think we are listening, but we are not actually *hearing*. We are not internalizing the message.

I was reading a book called "P.E.T. Parent Effectiveness Training," by Dr. Thomas Gordon. He teaches the skills we need to show our children that we are actually listening to them. This includes active listening and passive listening. You repeat what your children are saying in your own words, to show them that you understood.

I decided to try this on my husband. After a lengthy conversation, I repeated what he had said in different words. I actually felt rather foolish, but I was shocked at his reaction. "Whoa - after all these years, you actually heard what I said?" This was a great revelation to me, because I always thought I *was* listening to him. Apparently not. It's never too late to start practicing good habits with your spouse.

When the great Rabbi Elozor ben Azaria was asked to be the head of the Sanhedrin, he was only 18 years old. He told them "First I must consult with my wife." We can't say that the holy sage was hen-pecked or afraid of his wife. Just the opposite; in his great wisdom he recognized that she was on a higher level than he in Binah, in intuitive understanding, and he wanted her advice. She said yes!

Now just imagine how young Rabbi Elozor's wife must have been, if *he* was only 18. We are not told, but the amazing thing is that she was entrusted with a decision that was vital to the entire Jewish world of Torah learning and scholarship. What a beautiful message to all Jewish women. We too have been entrusted with this G-d-given gift of Bina Yetaira; an innate higher level of understanding.

Let us all hope that we will use this talent wisely, bringing true Shalom Bayit into our homes, which will surely result in global Shalom, ushering in the era of Mashiach.

Please Give My Husband Parnasah

When you hear a couple say they never fight, don't believe them for a moment. Either they are not telling the truth or they are not talking to each other.

A Jewish marriage, Kiddushin, with Hashem as the third partner, is a holy union and has its own set of rules. It always upsets me that many young couples look to secular magazines and TV talk shows for marriage advice. How sad is that, when we have Daat Torah, our own system of conflict resolution.

Let me tell you a story I heard from Amanda, a lovely young woman who lives in Ashdod, Israel. Her story vividly illustrates how a bad marriage can turn into a great one if it is based on Torah values. Amanda told me that there was a time not so long ago when her husband lost his job. They had no money and no prospects. They already had one young child and she was pregnant with their second. It was a difficult time for the young couple.

"I felt that not only didn't I love my husband, but I didn't even *like* him anymore. Things went from bad to worse. I lost my way in Yiddishkeit. I stopped Davening, stopped covering my hair and lost my Emunah. I wanted out but had nowhere to go. Where could I go with a big belly and a small child?"

Amanda was angry with everyone - even and especially with G-d. In desperation, she turned to Chanie Friedman, the Chabad Shlucha in Ashdod, and poured out her heart. They spoke

Chabad House in Ashdod

for a long time and Rebbetzin Friedman gave Amanda a copy of my first book, *Stories to Hear With Your Heart* to read at home.

By Divine Providence, one story in that book changed Amanda's life forever. Amanda read about my visit with my cousins Sarah and Yonatan in Jerusalem, a very special couple with fourteen children k"h and a two-bedroom apartment. In the book I described how one morning when her husband was leaving for work, Sarah accompanied him to the door and with her hand on the Mezuzah said, "Hashem, give my husband Parnasah, a good living, keep him safe and watch over him."

Sarah had learned from the Rebbe that Hashem gives a man Parnasah only in honor of his wife. If he honors his wife properly, the channels of Parnasah flow; but the wife must do her part and must *bless* him.

When our Amanda read that story, she began to bless her husband every time he left to look for work. He did find a job in construction.

"One time I was asleep when my husband left for work," said Amanda, "and I did not bless him as usual. I decided that I would do it over the phone and dialed his office requesting that they please call him inside from his construction job; that it was a very important matter."

Her husband was working on the top scaffolding when they called him to the phone. He came down to the office and Amanda blessed him that he should succeed at work and come home safely as always, and they hung up. Right after their conversation, the scaffold her husband had just been working on crashed to the ground. "Had he not been on the phone with me, he would have been injured or even killed."

Dear readers, this is the beauty of a Bracha and this is the power of a righteous wife. Amanda got the message and with their newfound understanding, their lives continue to be peaceful and blessed.

Stories about

Mikvah

The Mystique of the Mikvah I

What if I told you that you have the power to invite the Shechina, the feminine aspect of G-d, into your home and to become a part of your daily life and the lives of your family?

Would you jump at the chance? Of course you would... and there is no better way than through the observance of Taharat Hamishpacha. When we keep this Mitzvah stringently, we bring Hashem into our homes.

This mystical concept is difficult to understand logically. But we do understand and recognize that there are numerous *fringe benefits* that come with its observance. We will discuss some of them here.

During my travels and lectures on this subject, there will occasionally be men or women who will come up to me and question me, sometimes aggressively, about whether these Mitzvos are really in the Torah or "were they just made up by some male rabbis?"

No question is a bad question, so I try to give the best answers I can. First of all I ask them, "What men in their *right minds* would make up laws that forbid intimacy with their wives for twelve days out of every month?" I usually get a smile.

Then I explain that in the beginning before the creation of the world, the entire universe was a Mikvah Mayim, a natural body of water covering the earth. It was a purification process that was a necessary precedent for the creation of our world and for the first man and woman. A Mikvah remains G-d's vehicle of choice for purification and sanctification. On our holiest day of the year, on Yom Kippur, we read the portion of Acharei Mot which delineates forbidden relations such as incest, bestiality and having physical contact with a woman who has not immersed in a Mikvah.

On this sublimely holy day, when we emulate the heavenly angels, it seems almost profane to read about such immoral acts. So why does the Torah mandate it? - In order to teach us that the laws of Taharat Hamishpacha are even more stringent than the laws of Yom Kippur. There are no loopholes or shortcuts, every detail must be meticulously observed.

The Mikvah itself is prominently featured in connection to the purification of the Kohanim, the Priests. It is explicitly stated that only immersion in a ritual Mikvah, and *not* in a bathtub or shower, was acceptable for the service of the Kohanim on Yom Kippur.

Anyone who has climbed Masada will remember that even during that tragic time, the Jews built several Mikvaot and you can still see the excavation of the ones that were built on that desert hilltop. Taharat Hamishpacha is such an important Mitzvah that Halacha mandates that in the event a Jewish community is so poor they cannot afford to build a Mikvah, they may and *must* sell their Synagogue and even sell a Sefer Torah to raise the necessary funds for a Mikvah.

Health Benefits

It is a proven fact that Jewish women who keep the laws of Taharat Hamishpacha have a lower percentage of cervical cancer and other related infections than do the rest of the population. Medical science at first attributed this to the fact that the men were circumcised and their women were therefore protected from some bacteria. But the theory fell flat when they did a study on Muslim men, who are also circumcised, and found that their women had the same ratio of infection as the rest of the population.

A woman's uterus takes seven days after menstruation to replenish its protective properties, because the lining has disintegrated. If a woman is sexually active during those days, she leaves herself wide open to bacteria that invade her body.

Keeping Taharat Hamishpacha requires separation for a minimum of five days during menstruation and an additional seven days after all bleeding and spotting has completely ceased. It is only after those twelve days that immersion in the Mikvah and resumption of physical intimacy can take place.

Let's Get Physical

I have a theory about the above specific parameters and how they are relevant to today's medical findings in women's health and reproduction. But first, I want to tell you a personal story. About seven years ago, I was having breakthrough spotting that kept me from going to the Mikvah on time. I consulted with a Rav and he suggested that I see a gynecologist. When I explained my symptoms to my doctor, she asked me how I knew exactly when and how much I was spotting. I told her that Jewish women do a monthly, internal self-examination and I showed her the cloths that we use.

My doctor was totally astounded and explained that mid-cycle spotting is one of the symptoms that doctors look for in detecting ovarian cancer. "*If every woman in the world would do this,*" she said, "we would cut our rates of cervical and ovarian cancer in half." That's a pretty impressive recommendation.

Observant Jewish women are in touch with their bodies, we have to be. That's why there are so many reports of women who were able to detect uterine tumors very early and had a much better chance of recovery. I tell all my brides that keeping Taharat Hamishpacha does wonders for a woman's health – physically and spiritually. I also explain to the young women that both are equally important.

"I hope you can't wait to get physical with your husbands," I tell my surprised brides. "I want these feelings of desire to be in your marriage in five, ten, even fifty years from now." I tell them, "Hashem also wants us to feel this physical, mutual attraction. He wants us to be desirable and desirous of each other. Marriage should always have passion. In the Torah, physical pleasure is not evil, it is beautiful and proper and, yes, it can even be holy."

Hashem gave us the Mitzvah of Taharat Hamishpacha in order to endear us to our spouses. For those days that husbands and wives cannot touch or even brush past one another, we basically become "forbidden fruit" and you know what they say about that! This forced abstinence builds physical desire and ensures that husband and wife do not become bored with each other. Both of them *literally* count the days until they can be together again. Each month, after a woman immerses in the Mikvah, it is like the first time all over again. Consider it a G-d-given prescription for a passionate and loving relationship, because every month, every marriage is born anew.

The Mystique of the Mikvah II

A Whisper of Death

Immersion in a Mikvah is one of the Chukim, one of the categories of supra-rational commandments given to us by Hashem that we can't logically comprehend. That being said, it is incumbent upon us to *try*, and especially to try and find those parts of the Chukim that speak to us spiritually.

The Torah is replete with references to the Mitzvah of Taharat Hamishpacha, i.e. in Parshat Acharei Mot, Tazria and in numerous other sources. These crucial Family Purity laws, because of their sensitive and *private* nature, were not widely disseminated or publicized. Rather they were passed down throughout the generations from mother to daughter. It is only in our generation, with the initiative of the Rebbe and his Shluchim and Shluchot, that Taharat Hamishpacha is being taught openly. It is no wonder that fully 70% of our young men and women have never heard of Mikvah, but when they do, many are ready to embrace it fully.

A Potential Life

What happens when a woman becomes a Niddah, when it is her time of the month? It means that an egg had been released into her body that had the potential of becoming a new life and it didn't. It became the blood of menstruation. The woman is now carrying within her body the opposite of life, *a whisper* of *death*, a potential unrealized.

Judaism, at its foundation, has a deep reverence and respect for life. We are a culture of living - we do not celebrate death. When a person passes away, the Torah mandates a seven-day period of Shiva to mourn the life that was and is no longer.

The seven-day period of counting after the menstrual cycle is also symbolically mourning a life that could have been actualized, but was not. When a woman immerses in a Mikvah, it is also to remove that "whisper of death" which she can neither see nor feel, but which can still linger. She does not want to bring that impurity into her home and into her marital relations.

When a non-Jew converts to Judaism, he or she is also required to immerse in a Mikvah. Do you know at which point in the conversion process, the new Jewish soul, the new Neshama, enters the body of the convert? Precisely at the time of immersion in the Mikvah. Another rebirth!

A Spiritual Scrubbing

The Mikvah is the antithesis and opposite of death. The waters of the Mikvah are called Mayim Chayim, living waters, in which we briefly return to the womb-like state, the source of all life.

Water is life and we use it to wash away any intimations of death. When we leave a cemetery, we have to wash our hands ritually before we enter our homes to make sure no trace of the impurity of death has stuck to us. Likewise, when we awake in the morning the first thing we do is wash our hands in the same manner, to dissolve any trace of the deathlike sleep we have just experienced.

The Halachot of Taharat Hamishpacha dictate that a woman must not have anything on her body that would impede the water's purification; no make-up, no jewelry, not even a strand of hair on the surface of the water. The tranquility of the moment transports her back to the amniotic sac. She is born anew.

Deconstructing the Mikvah

The Mikvah is a ritually prescribed body of water that has numerous spiritual components. Even the *amount* of water in the Mikvah is evocative and ethereal. For example, in order to be kosher, a women's Mikvah must contain a minimum of forty Se'ah of water (approximately 600 gallons.) Forty is the number of days it takes for a human fetus to be fully formed; the number of years that the Jews wandered in the desert and the number of days that Moshe spent in heaven studying the Torah.

The most *famous* number forty, however, is familiar to us from the flood of Noah when it rained for exactly forty days and forty nights. At that time G-d took the whole earth and turned it into a Mikvah, thereby purifying the world for all time.

The Mikvah waters have to come from naturally falling rainwater or from an underground spring. Look up at the roof of a Mikvah and you will see that it is flat and contains a tank for the pure, undiluted, heavenly, life-giving rainwater that is the heart of the Mikvah. Ordinary tap water that is used to fill the Mikvah must pass through the rainwater tank so that it too, is permeated with holiness. In today's modern and often magnificent Mikvahs, we don't immerse in the rainwater or spring water directly. A separate cistern of chlorinated water is connected to the natural water source and immersion takes place in heated, filtered and crystal clear water.

Separate Beds

Keeping Taharat Hamishpacha has an almost miraculous effect on the intimacy between husband and wife. The custom of sleeping in separate beds during their time of separation is designed to stimulate desire between them. If two people are sleeping in one bed, it should *mean something*. It should naturally be conducive to physical intimacy. Couples should never have to say to one another, "Why can't you control yourself?" We should not want or need to control ourselves from doing something that is good, instinctive and natural in a loving relationship.

When both partners feel that the reason they cannot sleep in one bed is because they *will* lose control, then there are no feelings of rejection on either side. Just the opposite; they each feel wanted and desired. By keeping these laws they are ensuring that the Mikvah night will be the most satisfying and rewarding night of the month.

A young woman I know who had been married for six months called me one day and in an anguished voice said, "My husband cannot have relations with me." After some probing discussion, I learned that she had been sleeping in his arms the entire month, even during their days of separation. He was trying so hard not to become aroused during the forbidden nights, that eventually he could not be intimate during the permitted nights either. Men's libidos are much more sensitive than women's, but neither gender should have to suppress feelings unnecessarily. Sleeping in separate beds is the solution to that problem.

A Hole in the Ice

Jewish Women throughout the ages have always gone above and beyond in their observance of Taharat Hamishpacha and many are the stories of their bravery and determination against all odds.

Our great-grandmothers braved dangerous roads, lurking thieves, long distances, freezing weather and much more in order to immerse in a Mikvah. Sometimes it was a proper Mikvah, but often it was a river, a lake, or an ocean. Occasionally it was even in a carved-out piece of ice in subzero frigid waters. Here is one such story.

Years ago, a woman whom we will call Gittel came from Russia with her family and was able to arrange a Yechidus with the Rebbe in 770. When she showed the Rebbe a picture of her five children, the Rebbe pointed to one of them and asked for details about the girl, indicating that there was something special about her. So the woman told the Rebbe that years before, her husband had been exiled to Siberia because he was caught teaching Torah. She and her family accompanied him there and when her time came to go to the Mikvah, the nearby river was the only place.

It was in the middle of the cold Russian winter, but Gittel was undaunted. She went to the river, smashed a hole in the ice, immersed, dressed and went home. Upon her return, she noticed that there was a bandage still stuck on her back. She had forgotten about it and had not removed it. She decided that there was no other choice; she had to turn around and re-immerse in the *icy hole*. That night, she conceived this daughter that the Rebbe was asking about. The Rebbe told her, "It was because of your Mesirat Nefesh, because of your sacrifice for Taharat Hamishpacha, that you were repaid with the birth of this holy soul."

Today there are many women, particularly the Shluchot of the Rebbe who live in far-flung and primitive communities, who are still experiencing danger and difficulty in order to immerse in a Mikvah. Surely they too will be rewarded with special children and special souls.

The magnificent Sterling Mikvah: Chabad, Richmond, Virginia

The rest of us have it easy. We can choose from a variety of luxurious, spa-like and lavishly decorated Mikvahs in which to immerse. No suffering, no danger, no cutting holes in the ice.

Let's make that choice joyfully and thankfully and may we all be rewarded with healthy and beautiful children who will continue to keep this special Mitzvah for generations to come.

"I Think My Husband Is Cheating On Me"

For fifteen all-too-short but glorious years, I had the merit of receiving guidance, direction and Brachot from the Lubavitcher Rebbe in my work as a marriage counselor and Kallah teacher.

During the course of those 15 years, I communicated with the Rebbe about countless couples from every walk of life, who were having marital issues, fertility issues or were just plain unhappy.

One of the answers the Rebbe gave me quite often was to request that the women keep the Mitzvah of Taharat Hamishpacha with greater attention to every detail.

I must confess that in the beginning, I would ask myself how keeping these laws more stringently was going to change the tormented couple's lives; there were so many other issues involved. After a little while, however, I had no more questions because I merited to see with my own eyes how keeping this Mitzvah B'hiddur, strictly, brought about a miraculous transformation.

A Persian couple that had left Iran became very successful and wealthy in the United States. The wife was a gorgeous woman who was the envy of her neighbors. She lived in a mansion, had designer clothing, extravagant jewelry, a handsome husband and everything she could wish for. But one fine day, this same woman arrived at my door in tears and told me she was thinking about getting a divorce.

"I think my husband is cheating on me," she said "and I sense that more and more he looks at me only as a sexual object. I am feeling so lonely, so unhappy and so unloved."

I knew that despite her tears, this woman really loved her husband. I remembered the Rebbe's advice and suggested to her that she learn about the Mitzvah of Taharat Hamishpacha.

"But we are not religious," she protested. "My husband works on Shabbat, he will never agree to keep this."

"But you are a Jewish woman," I told her, "and this incredibly empowering Mitzvah was given to *you*. This is your birthright, your inheritance, yours for the taking; religious or not." Although she was extremely nervous and apprehensive, she agreed to try and we strategized about the best way to present this to her husband.

That day she went home and somehow found the right words. "Can we try to do this together, for just one month?" she asked her husband. "It will be very difficult for me as well, but maybe we can regain what we once had." Miraculously, her husband acquiesced, but reiterated it was for one month only.

"From that moment on, my husband began looking at me differently," she told me. "I no longer felt like a sexual object, I felt like a wife." There was a dramatic change in their relationship. The one-month trial turned into two and then into three and I am happy to report that all these years later, they are still together and still keeping this Mitzvah carefully.

Is Taharat Hamishpacha the answer to everything? I don't know. All I know is that it works.

The Four Mysterious Women at the Mikvah

Jewish women are called Akeret Habayit, the foundation of the home. Our sages also say that the Jewish home is called Barzel, iron, because it is strong, protective and indestructible.

We find an amazing acronym in the word Barzel. The four Hebrew letters, Bet, Raish, Zayin and Lamed correspond to Bilhah, Rachel, Zilpah and Leah, the four women who were the wives of Yaakov Avinu, the father of the Jewish nation.

We are the daughters of these four women, who were seemingly made of iron. They were not needy or co-dependent; they were powerful, dedicated, devoted and inspirational. Most importantly, they remain role models to us today.

We are fortunate to have myriads of Jewish women, both past and present, who modeled the essence of Jewish femininity and grandeur. Let me tell you a story about one of them, the wife of the famous Maggid of Mezritch.

The Maggid was a brilliant, unique and holy soul but financially he was very poor. His wife was equally holy and pious and she never allowed their poverty to stand in the way of performing Mitzvot. One dark, cold and snowy night, she was scheduled to immerse in the Mikvah, but did not have the money to pay for a carriage ride.

Undaunted, she walked all the way to the Mikvah and arrived very late and after hours. Shivering and frozen, she knocked loudly on the door, but the harried attendant, knowing that she had little money to pay, would not get out of bed for her and ignored her frantic knocking. Disappointed that she couldn't fulfill this great mitzvah, the Maggid's wife turned to walk home and began to cry.

Suddenly, a splendid carriage appeared with four beautiful, aristocratic women in the back seat. One of them invited her in. At first, she demurred, but they insisted, pointing out the late hour and biting cold. In the ensuing discussion, she told them of her predicament. Upon hearing she was too poor to use the Mikvah, the women gave her money, saying they were headed to the Mikvah as well. As soon as they arrived, the Maggid's wife jumped out of the wagon, paid the attendant, and immersed herself.

When she had finished with her immersion, she wanted to thank the four women in the carriage. She asked the attendant where they were. "What are you talking about?" was the reply, "there has been no one here tonight except for you and me."

The perplexed woman had no other option than to return home. The moment she crossed the threshold of her door, her husband noticed that there was an otherworldly aura emanating from his wife's face. The holy Maggid already knew what had happened to her that night, but asked her to tell him the story.

When she was finished, he told her that women's tears are powerful and ascend directly to the Holy Throne. "Those four women were none other than Sarah, Rivkah, Rachel and Leah, whom Hashem sent to help you," he said. "And they prevailed upon Eliezer, the servant of Avraham, to be their driver."

We are told that his wife conceived that night and gave birth to a baby boy whom they named Avraham. The child grew into a great sage who was known as Avraham the Angel.

We Jewish women are intensely intertwined with our source and our roots. We are firmly connected to our matriarchs because mothers never disconnect from their children. We are linked forever to that golden chain of their Mesirat Nefesh, their self-sacrifice for us their daughters.

As the holy Maggid told his wife, Jewish women's tears are precious to Hashem and we may not squander them foolishly. Hashem loves to hear our Davening as much as He loved the prayers of our matriarchs. So let's use our tears wisely. We should beseech G-d to send His blessings not only to our families, but also to all the families of the world.

Niddah Is Not a Mitzvah

This may come as a surprise to you, but being in a state of Niddah, spiritual impurity, is *not* a Mitzvah. It is an unnatural state of being and most rabbis and all the Halachot will advise you to make that status as short as possible. In my Kallah classes, I teach that our goal is not to be Niddah and that it is their obligation to end that period (pun intended!) as quickly as possible.

I also stress that they are not the ones to decide on their own whether the staining they are experiencing is Niddah or not. When we answer our own questions, we usually err on the side of caution and this contradicts the intention of Taharat Hamishpacha. Hashem wants us to be united with our husbands.

Eight Hopefully Helpful Hints

The following are some useful non-prescription therapies to avoid unnecessary staining and to help with fertility and conception issues. They are all available over the counter. They cannot hurt you and they might just help.

1. Take Folic Acid. It is a vitamin that is thought to prevent birth defects. What harm can it do to start as soon as you get married?

2. Take Vitamin C Capsules, 1000 mg, twice a day, after your period. It boosts the immune system and helps to stop staining.

3. A tincture of either Shepherd's Purse or Chasteberry does wonders to help stop staining. Take 30-40 drops, two times daily.

4. Avoid dark grape juice or wine if possible, since it can cause staining.

5. To prevent yeast infections, take probiotics, as well as Acidophilus every morning before breakfast. Or you can eat yogurt, which contains Acidophilus.

6. Drink Red Raspberry Leaf Tea to strengthen the uterus after childbirth. Zinc and Kegel exercises are also helpful.

7. Keep a *Jewish* calendar with Jewish dates and times to chart your cycles, because a woman's menses function according to the lunar cycle. When the months are shorter, your menstrual cycle will be shorter as well and vice versa.

8. Try to maintain a state of happiness, optimism and cheer. Sadness never helped anyone and in Chassidic terminology "Simcha Poretz Geder." Joy transcends all bounds.

May Hashem open His vast storehouse of precious treasure for all of us and shower us with His abundant blessings. May He bless us with children and grandchildren from whom we will have true Yiddishe Nachas.

Stories about
Jewish Women

What I Said to the American Jewish Book Council About Jewish Women

Several years ago, I accepted an invitation from the American Jewish Book Council in Manhattan to speak about my first book, *Words to Hear with Your Heart*. There were more than 40 Jewish authors in attendance from all over the world who were plugging their books and explaining why the JCC'S in the U.S. should invite them to speak.

Many of the authors were quite famous and had written several successful books. I immediately felt uncomfortable and totally inadequate. What's special about my book and what do I have to offer that these authors don't?

After about an hour of listening to the other speakers, I began to see a disturbing pattern. So many of them spoke disparagingly about Yiddishkeit and most told jokes that poked fun at the Jewish mother, mother-in-law, etc. You get the picture.

One of the authors said that during her research she discovered that "Jewish women have secretly been yearning to become rabbis, but they weren't allowed to, so they settled for second best and became Rebbetzins by marrying rabbis!"

She said this with such conviction that it took me a few minutes to realize that she wasn't joking. The men and women around me were nodding in agreement and I felt like I was having a really bad nightmare. I had to do something fast.

So when my turn came, I decided I would tell it like it is. I spoke about the intrinsic value of the Jewish woman, her spiritual superiority and her defining role in Jewish history. No one actually laughed, but the applause was underwhelming to say the least. I didn't care. I was not going to sit quietly while they were making fun of Jewish women just because it seemed to be politically correct.

After the presentations we all went down for dinner and I was not surprised to see that I was the only one who had ordered a Glatt Kosher meal in advance. I figured that everyone will now think, "This is proof that she really is one of those fanatics."

One woman from the JCC came over to me immediately and asked for my card. When she saw that it listed bridal training as one of my services, she asked me what that meant exactly. I told her that I teach brides about marriage, peace in the home, and Mikvah.

To my complete surprise she said, "I'm actually getting married soon and would love to learn about this with you. Do you think you could teach me?"

We made the appointment and she entered it carefully into her organizer and into her smartphone and we were both full of smiles. The evening turned out to be a resounding success after all. Mission accomplished!

P.S. I did get a few bookings as well.

Three Mitzvos for a Meaningful Life

Let's begin with our essence, with our roots as Jewish women.

The Jewish people are called Yehudim, from the tribe of Yehuda, and it is the name that our mother Leah chose for her fourth son. We all remember the story. Leah's husband Yaakov really wanted to marry her younger sister Rachel, but their father substituted Leah under the marriage canopy. Yaakov later married Rachel as well and he also took two concubines.

Leah was a righteous woman and a prophetess and knew divinely that Yaakov was destined to have twelve sons: The Twelve Tribes of Israel. She assumed that the twelve would be divided evenly among the four women. When Leah gave birth to her fourth son, however, she realized that she was given more than her share and she was both humbled and eternally grateful to G-d.

Leah named her son Yehuda, from the Hebrew word Hodaah, thankfulness and appreciation. Our sages say that she was the first person to properly thank G-d. Our core essence as a nation is gratefulness and acknowledgement that it is G-d, our Creator, who is the source of every blessing in our lives.

Leah internalized that message and we Jewish women, her daughters, comprehend it as well. It is our natural legacy from our mother Leah. The Rebbe told us over and over again, how crucial, central and critical is the position of a Jewish woman in Jewish life. Many of us heard the Rebbe say it, but how many of us actually feel it?

How important do we feel on a daily basis? How much do we appreciate our responsibility as Jewish women? I'm afraid that we terribly underestimate our own worth. Chassidus teaches that Jewish women have the same job as the Kohen Gadol, the High

Priest in the Beit Hamikdash. Let's consider: What were the tasks of the Kohen Gadol? On the simplest level they were a) lighting the Menorah, b) placing the twelve showbreads on the Shulchan and c) offering the Korbonot on the altar. Jewish women, too, perform these tasks, albeit in a different format:

Lighting Shabbos and Holiday candles is the equivalent of lighting the Menorah. The flames were meant not only to illuminate the inside, but also to serve as a beacon of holy light to all passersby. Our homes too radiate with the lights kindled by Jewish women and illuminate not only the rooms, but also the hearts and souls of our families and indeed the entire world.

Baking Challah for Shabbat and Holidays is in place of the twelve loaves of the showbread. We place two six-braided challahs on our table for a total of twelve, corresponding to the Twelve Tribes. Taking Challah, reciting the blessing and burning the piece of dough is an allusion to the Kohanim in the Temple and also a tangible reminder that we are performing a holy task. The Challah represents the entire realm of Kashrut and holiness in all that we eat and serve to our families.

Taharat Hamishpacha, family purity and Mikvah, is not a cleansing for the body as many people assume; it is a purification for our G-dly souls. The Kohanim were instructed to immerse themselves in the Mikvah before offering Korbonot, not because they were physically dirty, but to remove any taint of impurity from their Neshamot.

Just as the immersion of the Kohanim affected the entire Jewish people, so too when Jewish women immerse in the Mikvah, the purity and beauty of the Jewish family is maintained and affirmed. What a beautiful and holy job is ours.

In his well-known "Woman of Valor," Shlomo Hamelech, the wisest of all men, says that "Sheker HaChen," that charm is false and beauty is transient. The word HaChen has three letters: Hay, Chet and Nun. These letters form an acronym for the three Mitzvos of women that we have just discussed. *Hadlokas Haner, Challah* and *Nidah* – lighting candles, taking Challah and keeping the laws of Mikvah.

King Solomon is trying to tell us that if women do not properly observe these three Mitzvot, then of what use is our Chen, our charm? There is much to think about.

The Chassidic Connotations of the Three C's

G-d blessed our first matriarch Sarah with three gifts, which she then bequeathed to us, her children. As Jewish women we are all daughters of Sarah Imeinu, of Sarah our mother. We also refer to the other three matriarchs, Rivkah, Rachel and Leah, as mother.

This is not just a loving aphorism; it is a real, direct and transformational legacy that we have all inherited.

The Torah does not use the term 'mother' or 'father' lightly. In fact, throughout our history, that appellation only applies to the forementioned four women and three men: Avraham, Yitzchak and Yaakov. Their descendants, you and I, can access everything that they experienced and all the blessings that they were given, today and for all time.

Let's begin with Sarah. What were the three miraculous gifts she was given and how can we use those gifts to bring more blessing into our lives right now?

1. When Sarah lit her Shabbat candles, they continued to burn brightly until the next week when she would light them again.

2. There was a special blessing in her Challah dough so that it was always fresh, fragrant and plentiful; enough to feed as many guests as came to their home.

3. Sarah's tent was distinguishable by the Ananei HaKovod, the Clouds of Glory signifying G-d's special presence, that hovered above it at all times. This represents the mitzvah of Taharat Hamishpacha.

These three gifts from Hashem to our mother Sarah are accessible to us today. Here's how.

Candle Lighting:

Remember and rejoice that when we light our Shabbat and Holiday candles, we're not just kindling a physical flame; we are bringing an infinite G-dly glow into the world, into a realm of spiritual darkness that yearns for our light.

We know that on Friday nights, *two* heavenly angels accompany us home from the Synagogue, where we welcome them with the Shalom Aleichem prayer before Kiddush. The guardian angel hopes to see our home properly bedecked for Shabbat. The second angel is looking to find fault. When the three gifts of Sarah are visible and pervasive in our homes; when our candles are lit and the table is laid with the two Challahs and our beds are made, the guardian angel will bless us and the second one will be compelled to answer Amen.

We can do something every single day to bring the beauty of Shabbat into our workweek. When we invite guests to our meal, polish the candlesticks, or buy a special treat for our Shabbat table, we have already embarked on our voyage to the sacred seventh day.

Challah:

Baking Challah is both a preparation for Shabbat and a Mitzvah all by itself. It's simple, satisfying and spiritual. It's a Mitzvah that is really a joy to perform. When we separate the piece of dough and make the Bracha, we are elevating our food to a higher level. We are in essence saying to Hashem, "I know that everything we have is only through Your blessings and we are confident that You will continue to give us our daily bread."

The deeper significance of baking Challah is the concept of "you are what you eat." The laws of Kashrut are the domain of the Jewish woman, because we are the ones that Hashem entrusted to be the guardians of that Mitzvah. It is important that we continuously review and re-review what it means to be Kosher. And when we make that occasional error, *and we will*, let's not decide on our own to throw the food or utensil away. It's always advisable to check with our Rav first. By the way, baking Challah is also considered a Segulah, a good omen, for having an easy childbirth and other blessings. What harm can it do to try?

Clouds of Intimacy:

The cloud above Sarah's tent was an allusion to the Mitzvah of Taharat Hamishpacha. It provided cover, comfort and protection from the outside world and established a spiritual intimacy between G-d and Sarah.

Like the Heavenly cloud, the practice of Taharat Hamishpacha provides an intimate and private space for the loving expression between husband and wife. This leads to establishing a Jewish home that is modest, spiritual and holy.

In the merit of keeping the above three Mitzvos to the best of our abilities, may we all be blessed with light, sustenance and holiness.

The Rebbetzin Places an Order

Michelle was a 16-year-old Persian girl who had been saved from Iran during the Revolution. She was living with a family in Crown Heights who were kind and loving to her, but she was very lonely and terribly missed her family back home.

Michelle worked in a local Crown Heights restaurant answering calls and preparing orders. One day, the phone rang and a woman on the other end asked to place an order and gave Michelle her address on President Street.

When the woman gave her name as Mrs. Schneerson, Michelle suddenly realized with whom she was speaking.

Shyly, she asked, "Excuse me, but are you the Rebbe's wife?" The voice on the phone said yes, she was. Michelle couldn't help herself and she began to cry loudly. The Rebbetzin asked her kindly what was wrong and whether she could help her.

In between sobs, Michelle poured out her heart, telling the Rebbetzin how much she missed her parents and how hard it was to make a new life in America. The Rebbetzin stayed on the phone with her until she had calmed down, and then invited her to visit at her home, saying that she would always be welcome.

Michelle, who is a happily married mother today, was blushing badly at this part of the story. "How could I have done that?" she said to me. "But I felt that the Rebbetzin really cared and she was so easy to talk to."

Every time I see Michelle, I remember this story. It always inspires me to try and make time to be kind to everyone we encounter. The Rebbetzin Chaya Mushkah was a shining example for all of us to emulate.

Have Faith Will Travel

My dear sister who lives in the Old City of Jerusalem told me the following story.

One of her neighbors, Naomi, very much wanted to attend the annual N'shei Chabad convention which was being held in New York. She had heard that it was one of the most inspirational events of the year and she desperately wanted to be there.

Her practical husband pointed out that they were already struggling financially, as are so many families who live there. He reminded her that they were barely managing their basic everyday expenses; how would they pay for a ticket to the U.S.?

Naomi was not about to be dissuaded. She confidently packed a suitcase and placed it by the front door. "I have faith that somehow, Hashem will find a way for me to go."

A few days later, on a lovely Jerusalem evening, the couple sat down to enjoy a glass of tea. Suddenly, there was a knock on the door. When her husband went to see who it was, he found a member of their community holding an envelope in his hand and wearing a big smile on his face. "We heard that your wife really wanted to go to the Convention, so your friends got together and we raised the money for the ticket. Here it is and please wish her a wonderful trip."

Naomi of course was ecstatic. "Hashem has heard my prayers!" she exclaimed. "But how can you go to America without a dollar in your pocket?" asked her ever-practical husband. "Hashem has already given us this much, He will surely take care of everything else," Naomi said serenely.

As they were speaking, there was another knock on the door. In walked a friend whom they had not seen in years. He seemed terribly embarrassed and was actually blushing. "You remember how you lent me $2,000 two years ago when I had no way of paying you back? Well, now I have it and I want to thank you not only for the loan, but especially for not harassing me about it. Here it is, paid in full. Thank you again for your kindness." He put the money on the table and quickly left the house.

Naomi's husband was finally speechless. Wordlessly he picked up the bills and handed them to his wife. "Here is the money which Hashem has surely sent you. Have a great trip."

Just an 'Ordinary' Jewish Woman

On a recent trip to Eretz Yisrael to visit my mother, may she live and be well, I stayed with my dear sister, Leah Halbfinger. My sister lives in the Rova, the Jewish Quarter of Jerusalem, which is just opposite the Kotel. It's an amazing Zchut to be so close that I can go there anytime I want, day or night.

There is a beautiful collective prayer gathering held at the Kotel every night, exactly at the stroke of midnight. I try to attend as often as possible to meditate and just feel the energy of the Shechinah, which is practically tangible at that hour.

One night as I was approaching the Kotel, my mobile phone rang and I saw that it was a call from the States.

It was a call from a friend who had been going through some unspeakable suffering. She used to call me from time to time to pour out her heart and weep bitter tears. As always, I felt pain in my heart at the trials and tribulations she was experiencing, with no apparent letup in sight.

I listened as she told me again, in torrents of grief, about her despair and bitterness. Sighing, I did not know what else I could say to her that I had not already said in the past. I wanted so much to help her, my sympathy was not enough, but what could I do?

On the spur of the moment, I said to her, "I am going to the Kotel right now. I will put my phone next to the holy wall. You can tell Hashem yourself what it is that you want." Striding purposefully towards the Kotel, I pressed my face against the cool ancient stones and whispered to the unfortunate woman, "Okay, I am here now; scream to Hashem for what you want." I waited for the woman's desperate demands, but she stopped crying and quietly whispered a tearful, heartfelt prayer. "I only want Mashiach to come." That was it! She asked nothing for herself, nothing for a reprieve of her horrendous problems. She asked only for Mashiach.

Hashem - how holy are Your Jewish daughters. You took us out of Egypt because of the righteous women in *that* generation. Please redeem us from this long and bitter Galut in the merit of *our* righteous women.

Miriam, the Prophetess of Jerusalem

In Yerushalayim there lived a lady, a true Aishes Chayil, who was a constant source of inspiration to me for many, many years.

Her name was Miriam and she was related to me both by blood and by marriage. She recently passed away at the ripe old age of 106 and my heart is telling me that it is time for her to be revealed so that others can learn from her righteousness.

During the course of her years, many reporters in Israel wanted to interview this remarkable woman, because her fame had spread far and wide, but she refused every interview. I am so thankful to G-d, that she chose to share some of her life story with me, probably because we were relatives. And now I would like to share Miriam's story with you, my dear readers.

Like her namesake, Miriam was a genuine Neviah - a prophetess. Although she was born in Iran, she lived in Eretz Yisrael for more than 80 years, in the Bukharin quarter of Yerushalayim. She recalled that when she was a young woman, the area was nothing more than a large unkempt field.

Here I am with the woman everyone called 'Miriam, the Prophetess of Jerusalem'.

Miriam was married at the tender age of 13. This was a common practice in her native Iran because it was to prevent Moslem men from proposing marriage to the parents of young Jewish girls. After their wedding, Miriam emigrated with her husband's family to Eretz Yisrael.

In those days, Yerushalayim was a besieged and poverty-stricken city and the young couple lived in appalling squalor. Miriam however, was unwavering in her love of Eretz Yisrael and would not leave our Holy Land.

Tragically, for many years Miriam and her husband were not blessed with children and they suffered the heartbreak of losing several babies at birth, or shortly thereafter. Miriam requested a Bracha from a famous and holy Mekubal, who advised her to undertake three resolutions:

1. To go to many Seudot Mitzvah such as weddings or Brit Milot and to wholeheartedly say Amen to the Brachot.
2. To give Tzedaka for Hachnasat Orchim.
3. To undertake a major personal challenge upon herself.

Miriam immediately followed the Mekubal's advice and for her personal challenge she took upon herself an oath of poverty. She sold all her gold jewelry, which were the only items of value that they owned and then gave the entire proceeds to Tzedaka.

As Miriam was telling me this story, she was ecstatic and her face was beaming. "Hashem accepted my bargain and we became so poor that we did not have enough money to buy food." She and her husband had agreed that they would never ask for charity, so she went into the fields to glean roots, berries and wild fruits. Her neighbors noticed that she no longer went to the store to buy food and offered her food of their own. Miriam of course refused and from then on she went to the marketplace with a shopping bag that she had filled with soil, so that the neighbors would think she was shopping.

Even with all this however, her miscarriages continued. One night, the unfortunate young woman was so distraught that she cried inconsolably for several hours until she finally fell into a deep sleep. Immediately she had a dream wherein a holy angelic figure threw bags of money on her table and said, "Here is the money that you earned from your sewing."

Miriam awoke with a start and realized she had just received a message from Hashem that she should begin sewing in order to earn a living. With great joy she told her husband, who asked, "How will you do that; we don't even have a sewing machine?"

At that very moment her doorbell rang and a neighbor asked if she could perhaps sew some new clothing for her children. Miriam told her she would gladly do it if only she had a sewing machine. "No problem," said the woman. "Take mine. I never have time to sew anyway, so please consider this a gift." Miriam accepted the sewing machine and began making clothes for her neighbors and within a short time she had enough customers and enough money to eke out a modest living.

However, to her great sorrow, she still had no viable children. Late one night, her heart-rending tears again brought forth the same angelic being. "Look at the wall behind you," he said to her. "What do you see?" She turned around and, as if she were watching a movie, she saw two children, a boy and a girl, playing in a field. "These children will be yours - no more and no less," said the being. But be sure that for the first three years you do not name the child and do not dress the child in new clothes."

That year, she gave birth to a healthy baby girl and as instructed did not name her or dress her in new clothes. They simply called her "Yaldah" - girl. When the child was three years old she went to school and the teacher asked her name. For some reason, she answered "Bracha" and that remained her name from then on.

All was well until Miriam suffered another miscarriage and despaired of having any more children. However, the angel came to her once again and said, "Yonatan did not come this time. But next month you will become pregnant." She immediately went and immersed herself at the Mikvah of the holy Rashbi and nine months later she gave birth to a special little boy whom they eventually named Yonatan.

This boy is now the father of fourteen beautiful and G-d fearing children k"h. He is a man who is respected by all and I personally once saw a grey-bearded, elderly Chassid greet him and reverently kiss his hand because Yonatan is known as a very holy man. All of Miriam's many grandchildren are a testament to their very special grandmother and to her Mesiras Nefesh for having children.

The Vision That Saved Her Life

Years passed and Miriam was once asked by her family in Iran to come and visit them. Dutifully she made arrangements to go, but suddenly became deathly ill. The doctors despaired for her life.

That night Miriam had a dream. She saw another holy being with a shining face and pure white clothing, telling her, "You must not leave this Holy Land; cancel your journey and I will stay with you and protect you from harm." She woke up with a start, and immediately canceled her trip. Miraculously she fully recovered her health and had no further problems.

Miriam continued to be visited by this holy being whom she believed to be Eliyahu Hanavi, the prophet Elijah. Many predictions were revealed to her and they have all come true.

On my last visit with her in Eretz Yisrael, I was privileged to accompany her to Shul on Shabbos. At age 95 Miriam had the agility and energy of a young woman. She literally ran down the street and up the stairs to the women's section of a picturesque Shul she had been attending for many years. After we finished Davening,

Miriam apologized for not speaking to me at all while we were in Shul. She explained that as a young bride and newly arrived in Eretz Yisrael, she was once laughing with some of her friends in Shul. Her father-in-law later admonished her and said that it was unseemly for men to hear a woman's voice while Davening. Since then, for more than 90 years (!) Miriam had never once spoken in Shul other than in prayer. I personally merited to see the Kavanah with which she answered "Amen, Y'hei Sh'mei Rabbah." It was as if she were literally standing before Hashem's Throne.

Every facet of Miriam's life was imbued with holiness. She was a dedicated member of the Chevra Kadisha and countless other Chessed organizations. Although she still cooked on a primitive primus stove, she always had plenty of food for unexpected guests and regularly gave food to the poor. Anyone who entered her modest home was showered with many tasty gifts that she begged them to accept because it would make her happy.

Miriam was also a living example of true Tznius. Her head coverings and clothing were always beautifully modest and appropriate. Many are the Mitzvos that Miriam performed anonymously and in secret. She went into the fields, picked cotton and made them into wicks. She would then wind each one around seven times on her hands and use them for her Shabbos candles. I am fortunate to have Miriam's special wicks and I light my own olive oil Neiros with them.

They are very precious to me and I would gladly share them with anyone who is interested.

One time, I offered to give Miriam some money for something she needed and as usual, she refused. With her beautiful smile she pointed to Heaven and said, "Don't worry, I have a great Banker." Another time, we spoke about the topic of Mashiach and she solemnly and firmly assured me in a reverent voice that Mashiach is indeed here; he just has to be revealed. Her face shone with a brilliant light and I felt dazzled when I looked into her eyes, they were so penetrating and wise.

The Torah tells us that "In the merit of Nashim Tzidkaniot we were redeemed from Egypt" and in the merit of the kind deeds of this special woman, Miriam Bat Esther Betzalel, who Davened constantly and wholeheartedly for Mashiach, may we be redeemed from this long Golus now. May her memory be for a blessing!

It Happened at Bergdorf-Goodman

Dena was a lovely young woman who attended our Chabad House in Queens. She had become a Baalat Teshuva and looked forward to getting married and starting her own Jewish home. She began the dating process seriously, but it was not working out and none of the Shidduchim suggested to her turned out to be her Bashert. Dena was starting to become sad and despondent.

One early spring afternoon, a woman walked over to the Clinique counter at the Bergdorf-Goodman Department store in New York where Dena worked and asked where she could find "kosher for Passover" cosmetics. The salesgirl suggested that she go over and ask Dena who would know the answer "because she's religious."

The woman looked at Dena and in a friendly tone of voice said, "You don't look religious to me." Dena got a little upset and asked, "Why not?" "Well...to tell you the truth, you're not dressed like someone religious."

The words hit Dena like a ton of bricks, but she got neither insulted nor hurt. She immediately internalized the message. "This woman is absolutely right, I *don't* look religious; my dress is inappropriate for an observant Jewish woman. My outside doesn't match my new inside."

Dena made a decision right there at the cosmetics counter at Bergdorf's that she would dress the part. She began covering her collarbone, elbows and knees and her new wardrobe was both fully Tznius *and* lovely. When I next saw Dena in shul on Shabbos, I told her how lovely she looked and it was then that she shared this story with me. Was it coincidental that just a few months later she met her Bashert and became a bride?

After their wedding, the young couple moved to Minnesota. All was well in the marriage except to their great disappointment, they were not blessed with a child.

Dena remained hopeful and thought it was due to her age, since she was a bit older than the average bride. One evening she was scheduled to immerse in the Mikvah, but the weather was ominous. There was a fierce Minnesota blizzard raging outside and her husband was returning from a business trip later that night and was unavailable to drive her.

Poor Dena was in a quandary. She was new to the area and a novice in snowstorm driving. She was from Tel Aviv where she had never even *seen* snow, let alone driven in it. She thought about postponing her immersion for the following night.

But then she remembered the Kallah classes she had taken with me, where I taught that one should never postpone the Mikvah night. So Dena bravely got in her car and set out for the Mikvah which was in a Shul a few miles away.

It didn't take her long (in those pre-GPS days) to get hopelessly lost in the storm. She was getting nervous and slightly disoriented when she heard the wailing siren of a police car pulling her over.

The policeman started to shout at her. "Lady, you are driving the wrong way on a one-way street; license and registration please." Dena lowered her head and mumbled, "I'm sorry, but I don't have either one."

By now the policeman was turning purple and Dena burst into tears. "Please, sir I'm just trying to get to the synagogue and I am so lost." At these words, the policeman's entire demeanor changed. "Oh, I know where that is, don't worry I'll get you there safely, just follow me!"

The officer was as good as his word and gave her an escort all the way to the Mikvah, without so much as a citation or a summons. But Dena's real reward followed soon after that. She conceived and gave birth to a beautiful baby girl who is the light of their lives.

Hashem tests us every day in every way, but He also gives us the strength and capacity to pass those tests with flying colors. We need only to follow His instructions with determination and courage and let no one deter us from our path.

Miryam the Beautiful

I would like to tell you the story of my beloved mother, Mrs. Miryam Solemani a"h, because she was a true Jewish heroine of our time and I believe we can all draw much-needed inspiration from her life.

My mother was born in 1926 in the town of Mashad, Iran. Her parents were Reb Yaakov and Chana Kelaty. The family later moved to Tashkent, Uzbekistan, where her wealthy father owned several fabric stores. The Bolsheviks turned their lives upside down, however, and when they came to power, my family had to flee for their lives, leaving all their possessions behind.

The engagement photo of my mother, Miryam (Kelaty) Solemani. She was 15 years old.

Their destination was Eretz Yisrael - with a stop on the way in Turkey - where they lived for a few years. While there, my mother became the family breadwinner at the tender age of eight. She was the one who would hold the huge tray of chocolates that her father was selling at the market. She was so beautiful that people put down money without taking any chocolates, so captivated were they by this tender young beauty. Her father was even offered business opportunities, if he would agree to put her photo on the boxes of the chocolates, but he always refused.

My mother remained exceptionally beautiful all of her life and her nickname - up until the day she passed away - was "Miryam Hayafa," Miryam the Beautiful. My mother's beauty was not only external; it reflected the inner beauty that was within, because she was known for her kind deeds, dignity of speech and modest conduct.

Eventually the family was able to move to Eretz Yisrael, or Palestine as it was called during those dark days. The British were in power and would regularly arrest Jews for the crime of being illegal, and my family members were arrested as well, but were eventually released. The British severely restricted immigration into Israel, despite the fact that Jews were fleeing from anti-Semitism, and persecution. Many Jews in Israel at that time had no choice but to enter the country illegally in order to save their lives.

Rachel and Rachamim Kashi, my maternal great-grandparents.

My grandfather, Reb Yaakov, was now reduced to poverty. Although he had been living in great wealth in Russia, he was ecstatic to be living in the Holy Land. He had a large family, eight children from his first wife and four daughters (including my mother) from his second.

My mother was married at the young age of fifteen to my dear father, Shmuel Solemani a"h, also from a Mashad community. He had moved to India where he had become a successful businessman, but where it was difficult for a Jewish man to find a Shidduch. So he went to Israel in search of a bride, where he met and married my mother.

India

Their first child, my brother Pinchas, was born in Israel, but the family later moved again. This time it was to Bombay (Mumbai) India, for my father's business. My father had done very well in India in the carpet business and was quite wealthy by then; he even sold carpets to the Maharaja of Jaipur.

In India my mother gave birth to my sister Laya, to me, to Rachel and to Akiva. She also gave birth to a beautiful, chubby baby boy she named Elisha, but he sadly passed away of jaundice at the age of two. This tragedy made my mother determined to leave

India. She wanted to move back to Israel, but for various reasons, they ended up in London instead.

India was not the healthiest place to live or to bring up children, but in some ways it was easier. There were countless "ayahs," servants who did all the housework and my mother had more time to pursue her Chessed activities. My mother also told me how impressed she was with the Jewish Mashadi women in Bombay. She said that they all observed many Jewish customs and the Mitzvos of Taharat Hamishpacha and Kashrut. The women organized many charitable events and my mother was often the leader of those programs. She was never happier than when she was helping a fellow Jew.

That said, my mother rejoiced when we left India. She was glad to be raising her children in a country where the streets were clean and didn't smell horribly; where there was real plumbing, and where the poverty and heat were not overpowering. Years later, I made a trip to my homeland and was so inspired by the self-sacrifice of the holy Shluchim who lived in much the same conditions. (Of course the Jewish world will never forget the ultimate sacrifice of Rabbi Gabi and Rivkah Holzberg, Hashem Yikom Damam, who were murdered in their own Chabad House al Kiddush Hashem.)

Life in England

We moved to Stamford Hill in London, which was near to the soon-to-be-built Lubavitch Foundation. In England my mother gave birth to her sixth child, my sister Chana. Large families like ours were a rarity at that time, especially in England, but my parents were G-d fearing Jews and lived a kosher life.

In England my mother worked hard raising all of us and keeping our home tidy and organized. She cooked and baked like a gourmet chef and was famous for her delicious meals. For Pesach my mother would start preparing at least two months in advance. She would paint the kitchen walls herself and make all the food from scratch. She wouldn't allow anyone else to do these chores because she was afraid they wouldn't be done according to her high standards.

My mother also taught all her daughters how to run a Jewish home. I realized later in life that my mother had unique parenting skills. She never scolded us, she just told us quietly what was right. She took great pride in her children and always showered us with compliments and love. We felt that we wanted to be well behaved, because we didn't want to disappoint her or lower the high esteem in which she held all of us. The glowing look we saw in her eyes when she looked at us spoke volumes.

How to Be a Good Wife

One of the most important lessons my mother taught her daughters, just by example, was how to be a good wife. My mother would stop her cooking and household chores before my father came home. She would change her clothes if necessary, put on some lipstick and sit down on the couch looking as if she had done nothing but pamper herself all day. She always wanted to look pretty for her husband! She always spoke to my father with respect. Until the last days of his life my father always said, "No one is more beautiful than my Miryam Hayafa."

My mother inspired respect in all who knew her because of her quiet dignity and wisdom. She spoke English fluently as well as Hebrew, Persian, Indian and Turkish. She was very modest in her manner, clothing and conduct and never boasted of her accomplishments. My mother was my Kallah teacher. She would tell me very firmly, "Sarah, if we could keep Taharat Hamishpacha in India, in that Mikvah, surely you can keep it here." This inspired me all my life. I have found everything she taught me to be absolutely correct; she even taught me the Chumrot, the stringencies.

'She Opens Her Hand to the Poor'

Although my mother dedicated herself first and foremost to her husband and children, she was extremely active in the Mashadi Women's Jewish League. She worked very hard to raise money for the poverty stricken old-age home in Israel, which had been founded by her mother Chana, who had passed away in Israel. My grandmother was known for distributing Pushkas, collecting the money and donating it to the Bet Imahot, the senior center. She also used to go every day to help cook and take care of some of the patients.

In those days there were very primitive cooking facilities and no modern amenities. I remember how my mother and grandmother would ask us to help the elderly women. They gave us teapots filled with water and we would let the patients drink through the spout because they were too infirm or too ill to sit up and drink. Imagine the relief when you are thirsty, but too frail to get a drink of water.

I remember going with my mother to the old, very depressing building, before the new one was built. They were such lonely, sad, elderly ladies who had no one to take care of them. My mother would sing cheerful songs and even dance for them – anything to boost their spirits. They loved her dearly and impatiently awaited her visits.

Back to the Holy Land
My parents made Aliyah almost thirty-five years ago, once all of their children were married and independent. In Israel, my mother promptly returned to her passion; helping the Jewish people. She was voted on to the board of the Mashadi community, a position she retained for the rest of her life. She was also on the board of a free-loan fund and many times she would take me with her on her rounds when I visited.

One incident remains vivid and indelible in my memory. There was a line of people waiting to apply for loans and one man had come to ask for money for his daughter's wedding. One of the women on the board asked what collateral he could offer. "Sorry, I have nothing," the unfortunate man practically whispered. "So give us your wife's jewelry," snapped the lady. My mother immediately intervened, saying quietly, "Do not shame him, give him the loan. I will vouch for him." He got the loan. My mother always had sympathy for the downtrodden and helped them as much as she could.

There was one Bukharian couple, Boris and Malka, who worked in the brand new Mashadi nursing home. They became life-long friends and admirers of my mother because she stood up for them so many times when they were being underpaid or treated unfairly.

When I would visit my mother in Israel, she would often send me with food to some needy families who lived near her home, as well as Shabbos food for her neighbor. This neighbor had several small children and worked long hours at a bank. She sometimes came home only minutes before Shabbos. My mother would say, "Take this food to her so she will not cook on Shabbos." My mother even spoiled her Metapelet, the home aide, whom she required in her later years, after my father had passed away.

Several years ago, when I went to visit my mother, she suddenly turned to me and said, "Sarah, I have decided to live in the Mashadi Senior Center," the home where she had volunteered all of her adult life. She no longer wanted to live alone, even with the assistance of the Metapelet. I was very upset, as were all my siblings, because we all wanted this special lady to live with us. Each of us gladly and sincerely offered to have her in our own homes and she knew we meant it. But to our great disappointment, she said, "I will never leave Eretz Yisrael and I want to be independent."

So at her insistence, we packed up the apartment where she had lived for 30 years. She could take very few things with her, because she was now going to be living in one room. But one of the very few items she did take, was a photo of the Rebbe giving me a dollar; that was precious to her. The Rebbe once gave my mother a big smile and complimented her on the Jewish education and Chinuch she had given her children. To the end of her days, his words stayed with her.

My sister Laya and I moved our dear mother into the Mashadi Senior Center, now in a beautiful new building with gorgeous gardens, in Herzliya Pituach by the sea. The Mashadi communities all over the world had contributed funds to build it for their elderly members who needed care.

The day we left the apartment for the last time, I was very emotional, but my mother was her usual calm and dignified self. As we arrived at the center, a large group of my mother's childhood friends - who already lived there - came out to greet her like she was a queen, hugging her, laughing and crying all at the same time. Even Boris and Malka came out to greet her, sobbing with emotion.

Although my sister Laya regularly went to visit her, travelling from Yerushalayim to Bat Yam every week, we hadn't realized that my mother had been lonely between her children's visits.

And so, Miryam the Beautiful blossomed there in that home by the sea.

The Final Years

One of her greatest pleasures was attending the Shabbat Services, which she had been unable to do because of her arthritic legs. Her face would shine with joy as she entered the Shul in the center. She never missed even one Kabbalat Shabbat.

My mother was known in the home as the peace-maker because she would resolve the petty squabbles that the women sometimes engaged in among themselves. On one of my visits, I was surprised to see a sign on the bulletin board that read: "Mrs. Miryam Solemani will be receiving today from 4-6 p.m." When I asked her about it, my mother blushed, but said nothing. Her friends later explained to me that anyone who needed counseling for problems would go to my mother for advice. The number of people who came kept increasing, until my mother had to establish limits and post her hours.

From a very young age I always remembered my mother Davening every morning. When she had finished the prayers, she would raise her hands up to Hashem with the following request: "At night, a fever. In the morning, death." In other words, she did not want to have a long, protracted illness before she died; she wanted her life to end while she was still active.

Her prayers were accepted. My mother developed complications of pneumonia and passed away the day after she entered the hospital, on the 17th of Shvat, 5770 (February 1, 2010).

My mother was in possession of all her faculties until the end. Middah K'neged Middah - just as she had helped the sick - Hashem helped her according to her wishes.

I got to her Levayah four hours too late, as I happened to be in Florida for a speaking engagement, and had to rush back to New York to get my passport before I could depart to Eretz Yisrael. And in Israel, funerals wait for nobody.

During the Shivah, everyone who spoke referred to my mother as Miryam Hayafa as she had been known all her life, for her physical and spiritual beauty.

I go to visit her often in the stately Bais Hachaim section on Har Hazesim, the Mount of Olives cemetery, where she is interred next to my father, right opposite the Beit Hamikdash, may it be built immediately.

We will very soon greet Mashiach and be reunited with all of our loved ones and with the great Jewish women - my dear mother among them - who helped to bring our Geulah. May it be now.

On the Road Again

> **Author's Note:**
> During the spring and summer of 2007, I did so much traveling, that when I required bunion surgery I considered it a sign from G-d. After my very hectic pace, Hashem in His infinite kindness was letting me know that I must relax and stay put a little. The following four stories are the result of that forced recuperation.

A Message From Gate 64

My trip to Israel to visit my dear mother a"h began inauspiciously. I was flying American Airlines out of Newark, an airport I was not as familiar with, and I found myself searching in vain for Gate 64. I found 63 and 65 but for some reason, I could not find Gate 64.

I finally stopped looking and asked a burly female officer for help. She looked me up and down in a rather condescending manner and said, "You're going to Israel, you people have to go to that area over there," and pointed the way to a screened-in, completely cordoned-off space. I realized that it had been impossible for me to actually *see* Gate 64, since it was separated and totally hidden from view.

I then had to go through security once *again* and I thought, how dare they do this to us. Why is this the only gate subject to this seeming discrimination? I was upset and resentful about the obvious security differences between travelers to other destinations and to Israel.

But then I recalled the teaching of the Baal Shem Tov that we need to see Divine Providence in everything we experience. I thought for just a moment and then it came to me. Of course there are security differences; we are a separate people. How can I even question that, do our sages not say that we are a nation that dwells alone? The security personnel at the airport realize that the Jewish people are different although they may not know why. This is something we should be proud of; we are not like the nations of the world; we are the chosen people. We have to be an example of goodness and kindness and morality so that we can inspire and impact the world around us.

Thank you, American Airlines, for that valuable lesson.

An Airport, a Defibrillator and a Kiddush Hashem

No matter how many times I visit Eretz Yisrael it is always so sad to leave our holy land. This particular trip was nearing its end and I was checking in at Ben Gurion Airport for my return to New York.

I noticed that over at the next counter there seemed to be a problem. A passenger wanted to take a rather large box onboard as carry-on luggage and he was trying to explain to the agent why she should allow it. He told her that the box contained a defibrillator because he was a medic going to New York in order to bring back an Israeli who was very ill and he might need to use it. Of course she allowed the box on board. I walked away and thought no more of it.

When we landed safely at JFK I made my way wearily to the passport control line, sleepy and exhausted after the long trip. Right in front of me was a man with his wife and daughter. Suddenly the man said to his wife, "I don't feel well, give me my pill quickly." She gave him the medicine but it didn't work; her husband fell flat on his face on the stone floor.

A small pool of blood began to spread under his head. The poor woman started screaming, "Heart attack, heart attack!" while clinging tightly to her teenage daughter. They were both screaming in fear, but no one came forth to offer any help.

I started to scream as well and then the agents behind the booth came over, looked at the poor man but did nothing to help. It was as if everyone was frozen! I burst out screaming again, but louder this time. "Help, we need a doctor. This man is having a heart attack!"

Miraculously, the very same medic who had been at the counter next to mine in Israel came bounding over from another aisle while shouting in Hebrew to his assistant to bring the defibrillator. The medic examined the sick man, listened to his pulse and heart, but heard nothing. There was no pulse and no heartbeat. The man was clinically dead. The wife and daughter burst out crying and I must admit that I was also sobbing like a baby, begging Hashem for help.

The medic began manual heart compressions and after what seemed like a lifetime, his assistant came back with the defibrillator. Within a few minutes the man opened his eyes and began to breathe. Everyone started to cheer and several people went to clap the Israeli hero on the back. I was quite shaken for a few days after this drama that had happened right in front of my eyes. What message could I extract from such a shocking event? One minute a human being is in this world and the next minute he is...

We all know that Hashem sends the Refuah, the cure, before He sends the illness. This medic had been sent to New York in order to bring back a fellow Israeli who was ill. That's what he thought, but Hashem had other plans for him as well. He was also sent to save the life of a stranger, a dying man in an airport terminal.

The Kiddush Hashem was so immense that morning. Hashem's chosen people are not only a light unto the world, but are also the healers of the world. We have the capacity to bring both spiritual and physical healing. By our actions we can create a true Dirah B'tachtonim, a spiritual home for G-d in this material world.

Rediscovering My Dad

I always go to Rachel's Tomb on my visits to Israel. It is always emotional for me, but this particular time I found myself in tears even before we arrived at that holy spot.

It is so sad that we have to use bulletproof buses to get there while non-Jews can travel any way they like. Our bus had to drive between tall granite walls with barbed-wire tops and down a long winding road before we arrived at the forlorn resting place of our Mother Rachel. Indeed she has much to cry about.

We had to wait a while for the security detail to join us before we could get off the bus and I struck up a conversation with the woman seated next to me. She detected my English accent and asked where I was from. "Actually I grew up in London" I said. "Where in London?" "In Stamford Hill," I told her. "In Stamford Hill? That's where I'm from. What road?" I told her it was Portland Avenue. "That's where I

Shmuel Solemani, my dear father, with my son David at his bar mitzvah.

live, what number?" When I said 32, she practically turned purple. "You're not going to believe this but I think we bought our house from your family. Are you related to Mr. Solemani?"

When I told her that it was indeed my father, I suddenly remembered that we had met before. Many years ago when I was speaking for the Yemenite community in Stamford Hill, I had gone to revisit the house where I grew up and I remember how this woman graciously showed me around. She was a member of the Vizhnitzer Chassidim and she expressed admiration for my speaking to women in the secular community and for the outreach work of Chabad in general.

She also recalled how impressed she was with my father when they bought our house. She noticed the devotion that he had for Davening with a Minyan. I told her that my father was famous for getting up at the crack of dawn to open the shul. He was also an excellent Baal Koreh and could quote almost any Posuk from Tanach. He actually knew it by heart. When I told her that my father was now interred on Har HaZeisim, she said that was very fitting for such a special man.

The resting place of my father, on Har Hazeisim.

How fortuitous it was to meet this woman again at Kever Rachel and exchange memories about my beloved father.

Inspiration From an Inscription

On this same trip, I paid a visit to a little shul in the Bukharian Quarter in Yerushalayim. The rabbi of the shul, Rav Pinchas Mukdassi, is a hidden Tzaddik of Persian lineage. The word for holy in Persian is *mukdass* and people who knew of his unusual piety and learning gave Rav Pinchas this name.

You can tell immediately that he is a very special person, humble and modest. His exquisite shul is filled with vibrant energy that is both holy and serenely peaceful at the same time. The synagogue is known as the Kabbalist's Shul, and Rav Pinchas is a master of Kaballah, having written many Seforim on the mystical aspects of Torah.

Rav Pinchas Mukdassi

As I looked around the shul, I noticed an interesting dedication plaque on the wall. The name of the deceased donor was followed by Hebrew words meaning "he left this hall for Hashem's hall," and I thought, what a lovely turn of phrase to describe someone's passing.

These words refer to our belief that this lowly world is but a vestibule to the world to come. If we want to go directly to Hashem's Heichal, to G-d's hall, we have to fill our lives in this world with Mitzvos and good deeds.

A profound lesson from a simple plaque in a special shul.

Notes Aboard an El-Al Flight

I was en route to our Holy Land to visit my mother a"h, as I did every Chanukah. Just checking in to an El Al flight is an experience. I saw both Rabbi Meir Lau and the Sephardic Chief Rabbi who were also boarding the overnight flight. I felt safe already!

My seat was in the corner in the very back row and after a while, I fell into a sound sleep. In my sleep, I heard the sound of a most beautiful Davening, so powerful and sweet that I did not want to wake up. After a few minutes, however, I realized that I was not dreaming and I opened my eyes to a wondrous sight. Ethereal angels all in white, all praising Hashem, were surrounding me.

They were in fact Jewish men of all ages and all persuasions, Davening Shacharit. The rays of the early morning light streaming in from the cabin windows reflected on their Taleisim with a blinding white glow. I was awestruck at the sight of Hashem's children serving Him with such intensity and devotion on an airplane.

The Baal Shem Tov once told his students that he had heard the Angel Michoel say that he would give up all his service and understanding of G-d, to have just one of the four Tzitzit of an ordinary Jew. An ordinary Jew, wrapped in his Tallis and praying to Hashem on an El Al flight is the envy of the angels in heaven! Mi K'Amcha Yisrael. Indeed, who is like you O Israel?

Eliyahu Hanavi's Appearance in the Channel Islands

I was recently the featured speaker at a Shabbaton held at the Channel Islands near Santa Barbara, California. It included a group of young Iranian singles that had formed an organization called *Roots*. Their goal is to inspire others to become Shomer Mitzvos. Rabbi Dovid Loloyan and his worthy Rebbetzin Ronit were the event organizers.

The Baal Shem taught that every Jew is as dear to Hashem as an only child is dear to a couple, a child born in their old age. Hashem nurtures us with love and kindness and just when it seems that we are about to fall, Hashem guides us back.

The group that Shabbat was made up of many more young women than men and when we got there, we saw to our dismay that several of the men who *had* registered, had not shown up. Now there were only nine men in total and we had no Minyan.

This posed a huge problem for Rabbi Loloyan, because he was still saying Kaddish for his father who had recently passed away. What to do? On Friday night, after a beautiful Shabbat candle lighting, everyone just waited around because there was no Minyan to begin Davening. The mood was gloomy and getting gloomier.

Finally I commented that obviously this was all Hashem's plan. This was happening so that we should search for another Jew who was probably in our hotel right now, a Jew who didn't know that what he *really wanted most tonight* was a Minyan. Everyone agreed and we immediately dispatched a couple of the boys to go down to the lobby and inquire at the front desk.

"Excuse me, do you happen to know if there are any Jews staying at this hotel tonight?" they asked hopefully. "Che?" responded the man behind the desk; it was obvious that he didn't understand the question. The boys then asked permission to look at the register to check for any Jewish names, but of course the clerk said that was out of the question.

Just as they were about to give up, one of the boys felt a hand on his shoulder and heard a welcome "Gut Shabbos." Incredulously he spun around to see a smiling older man clad in shorts and a T-shirt. "Are you Jewish?" he asked. "Yes, I am," was the answer. "We found a Jew, we found a Jew!" everyone started saying happily. The other men from our group came running and without further ado carried off the surprised and amused man.

His name was Eliyahu Rosen and everyone said, "You must be Eliyahu *Hanavi* who was sent to us because we needed you for a Minyan." Rabbi Loloyan was able to recite the Kaddish after all. Our group had somehow merited for Hashem Himself to help us find the tenth man. We were all humbled and awed by His kindness.

The joy at that Shabbos Davening was palpable. During Lecha Dodi the men lifted Mr. Rosen onto their shoulders and danced around the Bima with him joyfully. They also patiently guided their newfound friend through the Davening, teaching him when to stand, bow, etc. "This is the first time I actually understand what I'm doing in a synagogue," he said. He had grown up in a Reform temple and he remembered his father and grandfather as being "religious." Eliyahu, however, said that he had never experienced such a Shabbat or such warmth.

After Davening we invited him downstairs to share in our Shabbat meal. He told us that he was traveling with a non-Jewish female companion who was waiting for him in the lobby, but he would let her know that he was staying for dinner and he would see her right afterwards.

Eliyahu thoroughly enjoyed every aspect of the Seudah, even washing for the Challah. But most of all he was inspired by Rabbi

Loloyan's brilliant talks which he found interesting and illuminating. He even joined in the Zemirot, humming along as if his Neshama already knew the tunes. When the beautiful Friday night meal came to an end, we asked him to please make sure to come in the morning to our "shul" as he was our tenth man and without him we could not read from the Torah. But this time his answer was no.

"Sorry, don't count on me, I really can't help you," he said, "because my friend and I have to leave very early in the morning." Although he was deeply moved by the taste of Shabbat that he had just experienced, he had made other arrangements and could not change them. Our disappointed pleas fell on deaf ears.

Hashem, however, had other plans for this Jewish soul. Imagine our surprise and delight when the first one to come down in the morning was none other than Eliyahu Rosen. He was actually waiting impatiently for the rest of us; he wanted to tell us what had happened. He had tossed and turned the entire night, unable to sleep because he had been so moved by the Davening and by the warmth shown to him that he wanted to be a part of it again. He had changed all of his previous plans and was free for the rest of the day. We understood that this man's Pintele Yid, the spark of his Jewish soul, had been rekindled and it would give him no rest until it was allowed to burst into full flame.

During the Torah reading that morning, Rabbi Loloyan made sure that our guest got an Aliyah. Our boys again carried him aloft, dancing around the Bima. Eliyahu was in his mid-seventies but that morning he became a young man again. I could not help getting teary-eyed when I looked at his beaming, happy face and saw the Ahavat Yisrael that the boys showed him.

Eliyahu Rosen was back among his people and Rabbi Loloyan would make sure that he is back for good. As the Rebbe has said so many times, no Jew is far from his roots. He or she just needs to be "watered," to be drawn a little closer. This is our job as we prepare the world for the coming of Mashiach now.

The California Couple

Have you noticed that wealth does not necessarily bring fulfillment to people's lives?

There is a large and wonderful Persian Jewish community in California and I speak there quite often. There is also Baruch Hashem a lot of wealth in that area. I have spoken in homes where you need a mike just to be heard in the living room. But, unfortunately, even great wealth cannot solve every problem.

Take the case of Soraya and Isaac. They attended a talk I gave in Hollywood Hills and scheduled a counseling session with me. Soraya cried continuously during the entire one-hour session. Her husband was desperate; he could not bear to see her pain. "I am doing everything to make her happy," he said sincerely. "Financially she wants for nothing. I lavish as much money on her as she wishes, I am attentive to all her needs; what more can I do?" Soraya herself did not understand why she was so unhappy. She had health, wealth, a caring husband and a beautiful six-year-old little boy. But she felt empty and miserable.

Eventually, we got to the root of her angst. They had been trying for a long time to give their son a brother or a sister and each time they were unsuccessful. Poor Soraya desperately wanted another child.

I asked her if she would be willing to make great sacrifices to try and achieve that goal and she said yes, she would do anything. When they left my session, they took along a great deal of homework. I suggested the following:

1. That they take their son out of the exclusive public school he was attending and put him into a Jewish school.

2. To check their Mezuzot and Tefillin. It turned out that Isaac didn't own a pair, so I told them to call Rabbi Dovid Loloyan, the Chabad Persian Rabbi, and buy a pair from him.

3. To check their Ketubah.

4. For Soraya to take on a Jewish name, since her parents never gave her one.

5. The most important suggestion of all was that they begin keeping the laws of Mikvah and Taharat Hamishpacha.

About three months later, I was again scheduled to speak in California. Soraya called and asked to see me privately. I couldn't give her an appointment, but I suggested that she pick me up from the airport and drive me to the Valley, which she did.

I did not recognize her! Her face glowed with health and happiness. She told me that she and her husband had followed all my advice. On a recent visit to her gynecologist, he had suggested a surgery that could perhaps help her to conceive. "But I decided

I would go to the Mikvah before undergoing the procedure," she said. "Mrs. Karmely, I followed your instructions to the letter, and I became pregnant the first time I went to the Mikvah." I could only hug her tightly. I couldn't even speak. Such faith. She had truly opened herself up to receive Hashem's blessings.

"Just think," I said to her. "The Neshama of your baby was probably waiting to descend into your body for a long time. It was only after you immersed your body in the Mikvah that it actually happened. Taharat Hamishpacha is a channel for G-d's blessings."

Soraya told me she has begun inviting her large extended family to experience Shabbat with her, and entices them with a magnificently laid table and sumptuous food. Mitzvah Goreret Mitzvah. One Mitzvah brings another in its wake.

My Makeup Bag and the TSA Agent

Traveling around the country, or around the world, for speaking engagements is usually something I find enjoyable. On this particular trip, however, I was tired, hungry and cranky because my flight was early in the morning and I had just returned from a trip very late the night before. So I was not a happy camper when I got to JFK to board my 7:00 a.m. flight.

You can understand my irritation when I checked in my luggage and they told me I was overweight. I assumed that they meant my suitcase and not me, but I was upset. "You can either pay the extra fee or take some stuff out and put it in your carry-on," the agent told me.

Grumbling and muttering under my breath, I opened my suitcase and took out the heavier items such as my Siddur, Chumash, Tehillim, etc. I also took out my makeup and toiletries case, put them in my carry-on and confidently placed it on the security conveyor.

Unexpectedly, a brawny TSA agent approached me and asked me to follow him. "Ma'am, you have a dangerous object in your bag," he told me sternly." "A dangerous object? Me?" "Yes, you have a pair of nail scissors in there and you can't fly with them. You can either go downstairs and put them in your checked baggage, or we can just throw them away."

That was it! I had reached the limits of my patience. Both my tiredness and the insanity of the security regulations just caused me to flare up. I don't do that very often but this time I said, "This is ridiculous. A pair of nail scissors is NOT a dangerous weapon. Just keep them and let me go." The officer then noticed my Seforim and quietly asked me, "Are you Jewish?" I answered in the affirmative, wondering what he wanted. Then to my complete shock he said, "It's all the fault of the terrorists, Yemach Shemom, who are causing upheaval in the whole world. I'm Jewish too and I have a great respect for Judaism. In fact, I am slowly becoming more observant. Don't worry, Ma'am, I will take the scissors and mail them to you, just give me your address."

Dumbfounded, I took out one of my business cards that say, among other things, that I am a Jewish bridal teacher, and wrote my address on it. He took one look at it and said, "Wow, you train brides for their weddings? I'm getting married soon and I wanted my fiancée to learn about the Jewish laws, but didn't know whom to ask. Could *you* teach her? We would be so grateful!" Of course I said that I would be delighted to help.

All is meant to be and all is meant for good. I got my scissors in the mail and the TSA agent got a Jewish teacher for his future wife.

P.S. After that encounter my fatigue completely disappeared.

Four Stories, Seven Days and Nine Speeches in South Africa

My first ever trip to South Africa occurred during the waning days of the summer of 2008. I was invited by N'shei Chabad to speak *nine* times during the one week that I would be in that exciting, exotic place.

The actual visit to South Africa is almost more than I can describe. The huge Shuls, Jewish centers and Mikvaot in Johannesburg are truly impressive and are matched only by the unbelievable warmth, Achdut, kindness and hospitality of the people. Beginning with Mrs. Marion Dworcan, my very gracious hostess, every person I met was exceptional. Another woman, Mrs. Devorah Nates, whom I can only describe as a Mitzvah Machine, works constantly and tirelessly for Klal Yisrael. They both deserve a huge Yasher Koach and heartfelt thanks.

South Africa is beautiful in so many ways. The unity of the diverse Jewish population is truly inspiring and worth emulating. Mitnagdim and Chassidim, black hat and Kipa Sruga, affiliated or not, they all live together in harmony. The supermarkets are full of kosher foods and there is only one Hashgacha, respected by everyone! It is a truly inspirational country. May Hashem protect and watch over them and keep them safe.

The Light Guided Me Home

My next stop after JoBurg, as the locals call it, was a flight to Umshlanga, a seaside town that is also the home of the Zulus from Swaziland. I enjoyed dinner in the beautiful apartment of the Chabad Shluchim who impressed me greatly with their dedication and Aidelkeit. Their apartment opens up to lovely gardens and the seashore beyond and I took the opportunity before dinner to take a little walk. How very beautiful it was even in the dark. The aroma of the sea mingled with the perfume of the flowers creating a veritable paradise.

However, as I turned to go back to their home, I realized that I was hopelessly lost. From the beach it was hard for me to know which direction I had come from and I just walked up and down aimlessly. I was getting more than a little frightened when I noticed a light coming from a window ahead of me and I followed it. The light was coming from a large and beautifully framed photograph of our dear Rebbe, in the apartment of the Shluchim. I saw once again, and *tangibly* this time, how our Rebbe brings his children back from the darkness into the light.

A Doctor Tells It Like It Is

A beautiful young woman in South Africa told me that she and her husband were newlyweds and had decided to postpone having children for a few years. They consulted with a physician and he prescribed birth control, which she began taking.

The young couple was on their honeymoon in Amsterdam and were walking along the canals when she began feeling really sick and realized she needed a doctor. Just then they noticed a sign on a door that advertised a medical practice and thankfully there was a doctor on duty. When she told him her symptoms he asked her what medications she was currently taking. She answered that the only medication she was on was birth control pills "Are you married?" the doctor asked. She answered in the affirmative and then the doctor asked her a simple question. "If you're married, why are you taking these pills?"

The couple was thunderstruck; this comment penetrated their hearts and souls. They decided that day to stop all forms of birth control and welcome all the children that Hashem, in His goodness, would see fit to bestow on them. "It happened many years ago," she said, "but we still feel that this man was Eliyahu Hanavi, sent by G-d to give us this message." They were indeed blessed with several beautiful children, whom they are raising in the path of Torah and Mitzvos.

Spared From the Tsunami

I was spending Shabbos at the home of Rabbi Dovid and Chaya Masinter in Johannesburg. Their long table was elegant and hospitable and the dozen or so guests came from all walks of life. Everyone had a story. One woman came over to me to share an incredible experience. It seems that she and her husband were caught in the tsunami in Thailand and had been miraculously spared from certain death.

She described to me what she had suffered during that storm. She was swept out to sea from her hotel room and saw dead bodies floating in the water all around her. She didn't know where her husband was or whether he was alive. She recounted how she was able to miraculously rescue a tiny baby who was floating on a piece of plywood. Eventually she found her husband who had been taken to the hospital with broken bones, but who was otherwise well.

How did this young couple react to their ordeal? Their amazing response was to start living a Torah-true life. How beautiful are your children, Hashem!

A Ride on the Wild Side

My last lecture was over and it was time for recreation, relaxation and seeing the wildlife reserves for which South Africa is justly famous.

My new friends Devorah, Marion, and her husband were my guides as we set off on this adventure. First however, there were safety rules:

> Always keep the car in gear, in case one of the animals gets too close and we have to leave in a hurry.
>
> Don't feed the animals. Never get out of the car.

The long dusty road we were driving on seemed tranquil and safe enough but the ominous signs all around us warned, ENTER AT YOUR OWN RISK. To me everything looked peaceful and we encountered magnificent sights. A pride of lions and lionesses dozed peacefully just a few yards from our car. They looked at us calmly, unperturbed by our rudeness in disrupting their afternoon nap.

I couldn't help myself and against all regulations I rolled down the window and with my heart racing, began taking photos and videos. But no matter how many I took they did not do justice to the beauty of these noble creatures living in their natural habitat. Even their eyes were different from those we see in captivity; they looked both fearless and tranquil at the same time. We all kept repeating, "Ma Rabu Maasecha Hashem," how wonderful is your handiwork O G-d.

The circle of life was readily apparent in the wilderness. We saw lions feeding and leaving the carcasses to the jackals and then it was the vulture's turn, circling above us, waiting to pick off the remains. We were treated to so many glorious sights: A herd of splendid zebras enjoying the sun together with the colorful ostriches and long-horned rams. Numerous wildebeests galloped around gleefully and a cute (!) pygmy hippopotamus splashed in the puddles.

Suddenly we came upon a large cheetah lying lazily on the side of the road with its back to us. We quickly stopped the car and I again opened the window to get it on video. "Mr. Cheetah, turn around please," I murmured and as if on cue, he (she?) obediently turned its head in our direction. When we said "bye now," he languidly waved his tail. Good thing I have it on video or no one would believe me.

Just ahead was the only enclosed area with fenced-in huge cages holding the tigers and a few gorgeous white baby cubs. We were permitted to go inside where many people were actually petting the baby tigers. I was too scared. Watching a huge male tiger eating his meal turned into an epiphany for me. The tiger played with his meat first, tossing it up and down and then licking it before he ate it. He was so engrossed in his food that he was totally oblivious to everything around him. I realized there was a lesson to be learned here (in keeping with the teaching of the Baal Shem Tov), and I made an instant Hachlata, a resolution.

I resolved to try and eat for the right reasons. I resolved to eat to live and not live to eat. Not to simply give in to my craving for the food, but for the nourishment that is in the food. For the sustenance which permits us to have healthy bodies to serve our spiritual souls.

And in a final postscript, here is a notice that was posted in one of the supermarkets. "All loud customers and unruly children will be sold as slaves." Only in South Africa!

Coming Full Circle in Milan

Milan, Italy, is where my spiritual story began. When my husband and I were first married, we lived in Milan and we raised our children there.

After about nine years, I was fortunate to find Chabad and a new life, Baruch Hashem. I will forever be grateful to all the wonderful people who guided me on my path back to Torah and Mitzvot. To name just a few: Rabbi Gershon Mendel and Mrs. Bassie Garelik, Rabbi Moshe and Mrs. Yehudis Lazar, Rabbi Shmuel Rodal (my children's teacher,) Rabbi Omer Chizkia and Rebbetzin Esther Belinov.

They befriended me with a warmth and kindness that I will never forget. Of course this is all the work of the Rebbe, because all these amazing people are his children and an extension of him.

You can therefore imagine my delight when I was recently invited to speak in Milan and Rome. I looked forward to catching up with my old friends and I also carefully prepared my talks. I wanted everything to go perfectly in the city of my spiritual birth.

For the last year or so, I had been really healthy, Baruch Hashem. I didn't catch so much as a cold.

But on the morning of my flight to Italy, I woke up with a fever, cough and a pain in my chest. A visit to the doctor confirmed my guess. Yup, I had bronchitis. My doctor was aghast when I told him that I had to fly to Italy in just one hour. "You need to cancel your trip, you're pretty sick," he told me. But of course I had no intention of doing that.

I usually avoid conventional medicine and go to a Chinese doctor who heals through herbs, acupuncture and acupressure. But this time I felt I needed a quicker recovery, so I packed my antibiotics and off I went to the airport.

There was a young Iranian couple on the plane that was making their first trip to Italy. The wife recognized me because I had once spoken in her community. She had questions about certain family matters and I was happy that I was able to help her and also refer her to the Mikvah in Italy and to friends who would help them find kosher food.

When I finally got to Milan, I was a sorry sight to behold. I was terribly jet-lagged, had difficulty breathing and my fever was spiking. But Hashem in His great kindness worked everything out and I felt better the next day.

Visiting the Coliseum in Rome was a nice perk on a speaking engagement in Italy.

A few days later, I went to Rome to speak for Rabbi Yitzchak and Mrs. and Sarah Chazan. I slept throughout the entire train ride on the new Eurostar and felt great. I even managed a tour of Rome.

During one of the scheduled events, Sarah Chazan pointed out a striking-looking young woman and mentioned that she had never seen her before. As she was saying this, the woman came up to us and introduced herself, then shared the following story:

"This is the first time that I have attended one of these events," she said. "Let me tell you why I am here and what happened to me today. I was taking a little mid-day siesta, and I guess I fell into a deep sleep. My late father, who passed away three years ago, came to me in a dream, and in an urgent voice said, 'Rabbi and Mrs. Chazan are having a program tonight. I want you to go!'"

"The ringing of my phone woke me from that unexpected dream and I reluctantly picked it up. It was a good friend who wanted me to come with her that night to an event being held by Rabbi and Mrs. Chazan. 'I just had this dream,' I told her. 'My father wants me to go too.'"

"So, here I am. I had absolutely no idea that tonight's program was going to be about *religion*; I just assumed that it was going to be about archeology because that's my field. Now I realize why my father urged me to attend. He was concerned about my soul. I can't thank you enough and I really want to learn more."

The Neshama of this beautiful, young, secular, Roman archeologist was indeed turned on to Yiddishkeit that night. This is confirmation that no Jew can slip through the cracks. Hashem takes care of each and every one of His children and guides us back: lovingly, tenderly, and sometimes forcefully.

The previous Rebbe taught that in the days before Mashiach, we will be climbing ever higher, on the steep mountain that will lead us to Mashiach. At that time, said the Frierdiker Rebbe, we will all have to help one another to reach the summit. It has been a long and very tiring climb and we are so tired that we grab at any twig and stone that we encounter, no matter how puny or ineffective, for support.

Said the Rebbe: "We need to be those twigs. We need to be ready to help another Jew, even if we are but a tiny leaf, and even if it will impede our own ascent."

P.S. During my tour of Italy, I saw the ruins and remnants of the once-powerful Roman Empire; the very same empire that forbade the Jews from learning Torah and keeping Mitzvos. This is the same cruel and corrupt nation that murdered our holy Tzaddikim, including Rabbi Akivah.

Today they are just a shell, a has-been, forlorn and forgotten, but our holy Jewish people have survived the centuries of persecution and are Baruch Hashem still here. Am Yisrael Chai, the Nation of Israel lives.

Simcha
Don't Worry. Be Happy.

What is the Rooster Crowing About?

One of the first Brachot we say in the morning sounds a little bizarre. I know *why* we say it, but I probably never understood it because for the longest time it just didn't resonate with me.

The Bracha is the one in which we thank Hashem for giving the rooster the understanding to distinguish between day and night. Okay that's cool; the rooster knows *the exact second* when it is morning. But what does that have to do with me and why am I thanking G-d for this on a daily basis?

One day I tried to analyze this enigmatic blessing. I thought about the rooster. What does it do first thing in the morning, while it is yet dark outside? He starts to crow because he cannot contain his eagerness and enthusiasm about the start of a brand new day.

But why is he so excited, does he know that it *will* be a good day? Perhaps it will be a bad one. Perhaps it will even be the last one of his life, the day he is destined to become *chicken soup!*

It was at this point in my reasoning that I finally understood the connection of this Bracha to my daily life. The rooster does not worry about the outcome of his day, he is happy to be alive and is thrilled with the possibilities in just having another day. He can't contain his joy and wakes up at the very cusp of dawn to greet the new and unpredictable beckoning morning.

I am decidedly *not* a morning person and surely will not get up before dawn and crow loudly; it could even get me arrested. But I now see the wisdom in waking up each morning with a hopeful determination to *make it* a great day.

Baruch Hashem I have been given another day in His world, another day in which I have choices. I can choose not to squander this new day; I can choose to be kind to those around me. I can use this day and hopefully all the days ahead for good.

And of course I can do it all with Simcha and joy. I can employ the human way of crowing - a nice wide ear-to-ear smile. It's definitely going be a great day.

Enter Simcha, Exit Stress

On a sunny afternoon in Queens I was wheeling my grandchildren in their stroller when I noticed this sticker on the bumper of a spotless white van: "I am woman, I am invincible, I am tired!" I just loved it because it's so sad and so true.

The more progress women make the more burdens we seem to put on ourselves. In the good old days, which I'm old enough to remember, women were homemakers and dedicated themselves entirely to the home. There was no added stress due to an outside job or career. There was relative peace and tranquility in the home. The woman had her role and her domain and the man had his. But that was then and this is now. Today it is virtually impossible for most of us to get by with only one paycheck. But peace of mind and Simcha, happiness, is still something that money cannot buy and we need to find an acceptable balance. We do not have to become superwomen.

So let's talk about Simcha. Simcha makes our home the most inviting place to be. How we enter our homes and how we greet our family when they come into the home is crucial for Shalom Bayit. A cheery good morning coupled with a warm smile sets the tone for the rest of the day. I am decidedly not a morning person so I have to work at it, but I see the dividends when the day starts off on a happy note.

Coming home from work is usually stressful. At the end of a hectic exhausting day it is so easy to forget why we are working. Are we working to live, or living to work? I try to remind myself when I come home to put on a smile, no matter how my day went.

I have a little trick that might work for you too. Look at the Mezuzah on your door and see the letter "Shin" which stands for Hashem's name. Then try to look at it also as a "Sin," the letter that begins the word Simcha. In that frame of mind, unlock the door and enter your home. Feel the joy. Smile. It works.

The Baal Shem Tov famously said that Simcha Poretz Geder. Simcha can break down all barriers, all walls, all disconnect between people. It can accomplish even more than a river of tears. And besides, it's much more fun!

Stories about

Mezuzah

The Wow Factor

I was staying at the home of a legendary hostess during a recent speaking engagement. Sheila showed extraordinary hospitality and graciousness and we bonded over a cup of gourmet tea.

As usually happens, we began to talk about her life's spiritual journey, how she had come to Chabad. Sheila told me that during the 1980s, her husband had become very ill and at one point, the doctors told her he had only three months to live. She wrote a letter to the Rebbe informing him of this and asked for advice and a Bracha.

The Rebbe advised her to check her Mezuzot, and of course gave her husband a blessing. They found that several of the Mezuzot required replacing and/or repair which they promptly did. Her husband recovered and to the amazement of his doctors, lived three more years, before finally succumbing to his illness.

Shortly after they received the Bracha from the Rebbe, and had fixed their Mezuzot, Sheila decided to also go for dollars. When it was her turn, she didn't say anything at all to the Rebbe. He gave her a dollar and as she was walking away, he suddenly called her back and asked, "How is your husband?"

Sheila said she couldn't understand how the Rebbe knew who she was, but she was overcome with emotion. "That's when I decided that from that day on, I would cover my hair." And she has kept her vow to this day.

I realized that this is exactly what the Rebbe evoked in the people who came to see him. It was not to say, "Wow, he remembered me," or "What a great Tzaddik," or words of that sort. The reaction the Rebbe produced was, "Wow, I really should do more Mitzvos!"

The Smashed Mezuzah Masterpiece

"My mother was expecting a baby, and the pregnancy was not going well," said the successful and lovely Shlucha, who prefers to remain anonymous.

"The doctors told my mother to expect a miscarriage, because with all the problems she had been going through, it was highly doubtful that the baby could survive. My parents immediately informed the Rebbe about the doctor's dire pronouncement. The answer from the Rebbe was firm and clear: check all the Mezuzot in the home.

"Of course my parents immediately opened all the Mezuzah cases and took out the parchments to be checked by a Sofer. There was one particular Mezuzah, however, that they hesitated to open. It was an exquisite and expensive masterpiece. The artist had blown the glass around the actual mezuzah scroll, and the only way they would be able to take it out would be to smash the glass and destroy the case."

"They decided to have the other Mezuzot checked first and when they all came back 'kosher,' they had no choice left. My father resolutely smashed the glass covering, and opened the scroll. They were shocked to see that the intense heat of the glass blowing had burned off an entire word of the Mezuzah. They also could immediately detect what that word was: 'Levanecha,' to your children."

"And so they put up a brand new kosher Mezuzah, and, well, here I am," the proud Shlucha said with a big smile.

Stories about the

Baal Shem Tov

What's in a Name?

Our sages tell us that if a person faints, you should whisper his or her Jewish name in their ear and they will be revived. It's possible that a rose is a rose is a rose, but a name is not just a name. A Jewish name is nothing less than the essence of that person's Neshama.

About 300 years ago, the Jews of Europe were faint and fainting and they needed desperately to hear someone calling their Jewish names. Their suffering was endless. From the savage massacres, the pogroms of Chmelnicki (may his name be erased) to Shabtai Tzvi, the false messiah who brought them a glimmer of hope only to see it dashed to smithereens, the Jews were in dire need of someone to restore their Emunah, their faith in Hashem. And so G-d dispatched a *new* holy soul, a Neshama Klali, to speak soft words of hope into the ears of the Jewish people. His name was Yisrael, Israel, the same name as our forefather Yaakov, whose children, you and I, are called B'nai Yisrael.

He was known as Rabbi Yisrael Baal Shem Tov, the Master of a Good Name and his mission was to revive us spiritually to give us a breath of holy air, to comfort us, to teach us that every Jew no matter how far he may have strayed is and will forever be a part of Hashem.

Rebirth

The Besht, as he was known, was a descendent of King David and some say that his Neshama was the reincarnation of a humble and pious simple Jew who lived in the holy city of Tzfat almost 500 years ago. The story is told that one night, when this still unknown man had finished saying the midnight prayers, Eliyahu Hanavi came to him and promised to reveal the secret name of Mashiach. What he wanted in return, however, was to know what good deed this man had performed on the day of his Bar Mitzvah many years before. The prophet told him that whatever it was he had done was *so* exceptional that it had caused a great stir in the very heavens. The humble Jew refused to tell his secret, preferring that his reward come directly from Hashem. He had performed the Mitzvah for the sake of heaven alone and not for any personal gain. The purity and holiness of this answer created an even greater commotion in Heaven and it was decided that this man's soul would again be sent down to earth. And so it was that the simple Jew was reborn as the holy Baal Shem Tov.

They Passed the Test

The Baal Shem Tov's parents were the saintly Rabbi Eliezer and his wife Sarah. Before he was born, Rabbi Eliezer was tested by G-d. He sent Eliyahu Hanavi disguised as a ragged and dirty beggar to visit his town. The beggar flagrantly flouted the laws of Shabbat and no one would have anything to do with him; except for Rabbi Eliezer who welcomed the beggar wholeheartedly into his home. His love of G-d was matched only by his love for his fellow Jew. He had passed the test.

When Shabbos was over, it was revealed to him that he and his wife would be rewarded with a very special child. And so it was. On the 18th day of the Hebrew month of Elul, known as Chai Elul, Sarah gave birth to a son who would become the holy Baal Shem Tov.

Sadly, Rabbi Eliezer passed away when his son was only five years old. On his deathbed, he instructed his beloved son as follows: To love every Jew with all his heart and soul and to fear only Hashem Himself and no one else. For the entire year after his passing, the Baal Shem Tov's mother would take her little son to Shul to say Kaddish and everyone there delighted in his sweet voice. After the year ended, she too tragically passed away.

The little orphan was taken in by the townspeople who cared for him devotedly. They grew alarmed however when he began to leave the yeshiva and run into the surrounding forests to meditate and pray. After a while they finally just let him be thinking that perhaps he was a simpleton. As he got older, the Baal Shem Tov became a teacher of small children in the Cheder. He taught them happily with love and devotion and with joyful song. The famed Maggid of Mezeritch once declared, "I wish I could kiss the Sefer Torah with the same love that the Besht kissed those children."

A Radical Concept Brings Joy

The Besht continued his meditations in the forest and one day he came upon the "hidden Tzaddikim" who eventually included the young man in their holy work of self-imposed exile, wandering through towns and villages to teach Jews.

At the young age of 18, he introduced a new and radical concept to Chassidism. He celebrated the virtue of the simple, unlearned, G-d-fearing Jew who served Hashem with his *heart* and not necessarily with his scholarship.

He spurned the contemporary philosophy of his time, which taught that only the *learned* Jew could aspire to an elevated spiritual level. The Baal Shem Tov's message was a breath of fresh air to the unlettered and unlearned Jews who struggled daily to eke out a meager living, but at the same time, they served Hashem with a pure faith and a humble heart. Tens of thousands of Jews now had a new lease on life and a new spiritual master.

The Besht remained one of the hidden Tzaddikim until he reached the age of 36, when he was told that the time had come for him to reveal himself to the world. For the humble Rabbi Yisrael, the thought of fame was agony. He only wanted to continue serving Hashem in his own private manner. In order to make the proper decision, he abstained from food for three full days and when they were over, he made his decision. His answer was yes. The year was 5494 – 1734.

His whole life was focused on Ahavat Yisrael (loving a fellow Jew), Hashgacha Protis (Divine personal providence) and Simcha (joy). He would say, "The Gates of Tears are never closed, but Simcha takes you over and above." The Baal Shem Tov would give every penny he had to Tzedaka; he gave away every gift that he ever received.

He was sensitive to every person, but once he saw his wife combing the hair of a poor orphan girl, who was crying because of the pain. Since the grooming was for the girl's benefit, he did not respond to her tears. Heaven immediately informed him that he had lost his Olom Haba. Joyfully he proclaimed, "I am very sorry for the girl's pain, but now I can serve Hashem with no thought of reward." Immediately, his Olam Haba was restored.

The Besht's first wife passed away at a young age and he remarried Leah Rachel. They had a son named Tzvi and a daughter named Aidel. Although the Besht was renowned as a Master of miracles, healer of the sick and victor over evil, it was only a part of what he really was. He was proficient in Zohar, Kabbalah, Mussar and Gemara. He asserted that his great power of vision was achievable by all – that the light of the six days of creation was concealed in the Torah and that anyone who could extract it could see to the end of the world. He truly was able to do so.

He would say that Jews are compared to the stars because they seem tiny to our eyes but are vast worlds when seen from above. He made himself available to the simple Jews whenever he could. He smoked a pipe, carried a walking stick and would speak in their vernacular Yiddish.

The Besht once sensed that his Chassidim could not understand why he was giving so much attention to the unlearned simple Jews. He told his students to close their eyes and put their arms on one another's shoulders. He then completed the circle by placing his holy arms on two Chassidim on either side of him. Immediately his students heard the most exquisite, beautiful singing. It was the words of the Tehillim, but sung in such pure, vibrant and awesome tones that they almost fainted from the sheer beauty of it. It seemed to them that the voices were angels singing in the celestial spheres. Abruptly, the Besht removed his arms from his neighbors and they all woke up from their vision.

Smiling broadly he asked them. "Do you know whose voices you just heard? They were not angels on high. Just look out the window and see those simple, humble Jews reciting Tehillim with love and sincerity, those same Jews you do not hold in high esteem. Their voices are heard by Hashem in exactly the same way that you just heard them."

When Your Teachings Spread Out

Perhaps the most famous story about the Baal Shem Tov is this. Once, his soul made an Aliyah to the high heavens and in one of the chambers he saw Mashiach. "When will you come?" he asked him. "K'sheyafutzu Maayonasecha Chutzah," was the reply. When your wellsprings (your Chassidic teachings) will spread throughout the world.

The Besht would famously say that "studying the tales of the Tzaddikim is like studying the Ma'aseh Merkavah" and he taught many lessons from the myriad of stories he would tell.

Miraculous Missions

On his many missions to help Jews in need, the Besht would take his Chassidim along with him on his horse and carriage. He would tell his trusty Russian driver Alexi to "just drive" and he himself fell asleep. When he awoke, they had miraculously achieved Kvitzus Haderech, they had speedily arrived at their destination no matter how far away it was.

Many stories are told about these awesome missions that awakened the slumbering souls of countless Jews. Before his revelation, the Baal Shem Tov would immerse himself in icy rivers. Once a very ill non-Jewish peasant entered the water right after him and was cured. After that time, many sick and suffering non-Jews would immerse themselves as well and found miraculously that they too were cured.

Once the Besht went to an isolated field outside of Mezibuzh and Davened for a Jew who was ill. A spring of water emerged from that spot and to this day there is a well that contains icy-cold fresh spring water that is renowned for its healing properties. I know because I was there myself and took some water home in a bottle.

Here I am with a group of women at the Baal Shem Tov's Well. Notice the water bottles I'm holding, which I filled from that holy well.

The Baal Shem Tov loved light. Once during the winter his students told him that they had no more candles and that they would have to continue their studies in the dark. The Baal Shem Tov instructed them to go outside, break off the icicles from the trees and light them. They did as instructed and of course, they burned brightly. Tzaddik Gozer V'Hakadosh Baruch Hu Mekayem. A righteous person commands and G-d makes it happen.

The Power of Baruch Hashem

The Besht would delight in his mission of going around the country asking Jews how they fared, in order to encourage them to say "Baruch Hashem." Once he visited an old Torah scholar who spent every moment studying Torah and asked him how he was. The scholar, irritated at this seeming invasion of his studies, ignored his persistent questioning until the Besht berated him and accused him of denying Hashem His sustenance. Aghast, the scholar asked what he had done to deserve this. The Besht replied that Hashem derives much Nachas from hearing His children thank Him and acknowledge His kindness; a Nachas even greater than hearing the study of Torah.

It is said that the Besht learned Torah from the prophet Eliyahu and from Achiya HaShiloni, who learned Torah directly from Moshe Rabbeinu and was on the Bais Din of King David.

The Baal Shem Tov called his followers "Rayim Ahuvim" dear friends, but the Misnagdim (those that were against the Chassidic movement) derisively called them "Chassidim." The Chassidism thrived and spread throughout the world bringing much needed warmth, acceptance and love to the Jewish people, particularly the simple and uneducated folk.

Many are the profound teachings of the Baal Shem Tov. A tiny example is the following: In Tehillim chapter 34, we find the verse, "Sur Merah V'aseh Tov," turn from evil and do good. The Besht would translate it as 'turn evil *into* good"...a much higher level.

This was the legend of the holy Baal Shem Tov: To recognize the potential of each and every Jew to elevate themselves and their fellow Yidden. To serve Hashem with all their being in order to make this world a "Dirah B'tachtonim" a home for Hashem in this world.

We, the spiritual children of the Baal Shem Tov have to continue his illustrious legacy. His holy soul left this world on Shavuot, 5520, 1760. He is interred in Mezhibuzh in the Ukraine, where I had the incredible Zechus of Davening at his Ohel.

His mantle of leadership was assumed by his son, Rabbi Tzvi, who gave it over to the Maggid, Rabbi Dov Ber of Mezritch. One of the Besht's grandsons was the famed Rabbi Nachman of Breslov.

May his memory be a blessing for us all, and may we bring Mashiach by spreading his holy wellsprings.

Letters

A Few Words, Many Magnitudes

The following letter was sent to the editor of the N'shei Chabad Newsletter, February 2001

The Mikvah Association of Long Island will open its new Mikvah in Plainview, New York, in two short months. It is a project eleven years in the making and I would like to share the background story with your readers.

Years ago, I was a typical college student living in Queens. I was single and secular. One day I came across a flyer from the local Chabad, inviting women to hear a guest speaker in someone's home. The topic was "The Role of the Female in Judaism." To be honest, what intrigued me the most was not the title, but the smaller print that read, "There will be a free light dinner." Wouldn't that entice any college student? So I went, but not without dragging a friend along.

It was the first time I had heard about the laws of Mikvah. The speaker Mrs. Sarah Karmely so inspired and moved me with her personal stories that I made a mental commitment that if and when I ever got married, whether religious or not, I would consider following the laws of Taharat Hamishpacha. How could I have known that my mental note would eventually turn into both a physical and spiritual commitment and a connection to Klal Yisrael?

I had heard time and time again through readings and various speakers that keeping the laws of Mikvah is the secret to Jewish survival. It should not be a secret.

Since the '60s, intimate topics have not been left to the privacy of husband and wife. In today's secular world men and women no longer shy away from matters that previously would never have been discussed openly. The media is a constant reminder of this deplorable state of affairs and unfortunately the results of this [lack of boundaries] ... are empty marriages, divorce and disease.

Today's mindset, however, provides the opportunity to talk openly about Mikvah. The need to understand and follow these laws is more urgent than ever before. We have been given the chance to reach out and restore the holiness of marriage and intimacy...

So why is the teaching and learning about the laws of Mikvah still so hush-hush? The proven physical and spiritual advantages gained by married couples who follow these laws as well as the documented health benefits for a woman make it imperative that

Mikvah should not be left to the chance discovery of a Jewish college girl. Klal Yisrael depends on it.

My college days are long gone. Yet those stories I heard years ago still motivate me today. My husband and family now reside in Plainview. We are part of an established, rapidly growing, down-to-earth Orthodox community. I have been Co-President of the Mikvah Association of Long Island (MALI) for three years.

This past Shabbos my husband and I had some old friends over. After the Shabbos meal, my girlfriend and I began to put our children to bed. We smiled when we realized that both our oldest boys had the same colorful yarmulke and Tzitzit. As the children played we reminisced about the years when we were college roommates living off campus. We even recalled that day I dragged her to hear a lecture just to get a free meal.

In preparation for the opening of our new Mikvah, I am creating a flyer inviting women to hear a guest speaker. The topic will be "The Role of the Female in Judaism," and the speaker will be... you guessed it. None other than Sarah Karmely. This time it will be in my home and I will be serving dessert. College students are welcome.

Sharon Stochel, Plainview, NY

Dear Mrs. Karmely,

You were amazing! You have such a special holy power. In your merit, many Yiddishe Kinderlach will be born b'Kedusha v'Tahara.

It was such a Z'chut to get to know you and a special enjoyment in just talking to you. Your calmness and dignified demeanor are truly impressive. You are a real Chayelet, a soldier of the Rebbe. May you be blessed from the One Above with health, wealth, Nachas and happiness Ad Bli Dai. May we meet with Mashiach Tzidkeinu immediately in Eretz Yisrael.

Shterni Gruzman, Chabad, Vienna, Austria

Dear Mrs. Karmely,

Your wonderful stories, which are meant to inspire, truly do. Now I have a story to tell you for a change.

My husband and I have been married for ten years and thank G-d we have several fine children. We have always been Frum and of course we have always kept Taharat Hamishpacha. But over the years, what with the pregnancies and all, we both grew lax.

I rationalized that if my husband didn't care so much about the details, I didn't need to be overly careful with Bedikot, Hachanot L'tvilah, etc. Slowly but surely we were both letting things slide. We finally reached a low point where all I was doing was the Hefsek Tahara and immersion in the Mikvah.

As this was happening I saw our marriage going from bad to worse. We talked very little. It often felt like a marriage of convenience; we mostly talked about the repairs needed on the cars, the appointments for the kids and who was making the bank deposits or paying the bills. We hardly ever *really* talked and I was very upset about this.

After reading one of your articles in the *N'shei Chabad Newsletter* where you addressed just this issue, it dawned on me with sudden clarity that our problems were related to our laxity in Taharat Hamishpacha. I knew that if I cleaned up my act in this area, Hashem would help me in the other.

Soon after coming to this decision, the opportunity arrived to put my good intentions to the test. I cut my lovely long nails really short, I did everything correctly and didn't skip a thing.

Mrs. Karmely, what can I say? We now have what I had prayed for: a marriage that is a true union of minds, hearts, bodies and souls. We've been really talking and enjoying just being together. Our children of course feel the change and are much more relaxed. The tension in our house has eased up considerably.

Is Taharat Hamishpacha the answer every time a marriage is in trouble? I really don't know, but it's certainly worth a try because it's not as costly, painful, time-consuming or embarrassing as counseling. Also, in order for your husband to go for counseling, you would first have to get him to admit that there is a problem. In my case that was impossible. This was something I was able do on my own with just Hashem to help me.

But really, why am I surprised that it worked? Hashem created the institution of marriage complete with a full instruction manual. We need only to follow it and if we don't, we do so at our own risk. Thank you Mrs. Karmely and please keep on writing!

Bas Rochel Imeinu

Glossary

Achdut: Unity
Ad Bli Dai: Without holding back anything, without restraint
Ahavat Yisrael: The positive injunction to love one's fellow Jew as oneself.
Aidelkeit: A specific quality of character marked by a combination of poise and unpretentiousness
Aishet Chayil: A woman of valor; refers to the Friday night prayer by the same name
Akeret Habayit: The Jewish wife and mother who is the spiritual and material foundation of the Jewish home
Al Kiddush Hashem: (Dying) for the sanctification of G-d's name
Aliyah: Ascent of the soul to the heavenly realms; immigration to the State of Israel; being called up to the Torah
Am Yisrael Chai: The Nation of Israel lives!
Amos: Biblical prophet.
Ananei HaKavod: The Clouds of Glory which protected the Israelites in their journey through the Sinai desert
Avraham Fried: Internationally renowned Jewish singer and songwriter
Avraham: The patriarch Abraham
B"H: Acronym for the expression "Baruch Hashem"
B'hiddur: With precision in the performance of a mitzvah
B'li Neder: Without a formal promise and its Halachic obligation
B'nai Yisrael: The Jewish People, lit., the Children of Israel
Baal Koreh: An individual who is proficient in chanting the Torah portion in the synagogue
Baal Shem Tov: Rabbi Yisrael ben Eliezer, the founder of the Chassidic movement
Baalat Teshuva: A female who has returned to the traditional Jewish way of life
Baruch Hashem: Thank G-d, lit., blessed is the Name
Barzel: Iron
Bashert: One's divinely pre-ordained spouse
Bat Kol: An utterance emanating directly from G-d in Heaven
Beit Hachaim: A Jewish cemetery
Beit Hamikdash: Holy Temple in Jerusalem
Bet Din: Jewish court of law
Bima: The podium from which the Torah is read in a synagogue
Bina Yetaira: An augmentation of intuition to one's normal intuition
Birchat Kohanim: The traditional priestly blessing

Bracha: Blessing
Brit Mila: Ritual circumcision of a Jewish boy eight days after birth
Bubby: Grandmother.
Challah: Traditional Jewish braided bread eaten on the Sabbath
Chassid: Pious individual; a follower of a particular Chassidic master.
Chassidishe: Of or relating to the devotion of a Chassid to his/her Chassidic Master's teachings
Chassidus: Chassidic philosophy as a whole; often used with specific reference to the philosophy of Chabad
Chava: Eve
Chessed: Kindness
Chevra Kadisha: An organization dedicated to preparing a body for burial in accordance with Jewish Law
Chinuch: Education
Chmelnicki: Instigator of a bloody Cossack uprising in 1648-49 in the Ukraine which claimed the lives of many Jews
Chukim: Supra-rational category of Jewish Laws.
Chumash: Pentateuch
Chutzpa: Audacity
D'aat Torah: Torah knowledge in general; the opinion of an individual who possesses substantial Torah knowledge
Daven: Pray
Dirah B'tachtonim: Dwelling place for G-d in the physical world
Divrei Chaim: Rabbi Chaim Halberstam, first leader of the Sanz Chassidic dynasty
Dr. Thomas Gordon: American psychologist, author of *Parent Effectiveness Training: The Proven Program for Raising Responsible Children*
Eliezer: Servant of the patriarch Abraham
Eliyahu Hanavi: The Prophet Elijah
Emunah: Faith
Emunat Tzaddikim: Faith in a holy individual's capacity to intercede in Heaven on behalf of another
Eretz Yisrael: The Land of Israel
Frierdiker Rebbe: Rabbi Yosef Yitzchak Schneerson, the Rebbe Rayatz, sixth Rebbe of the Chabad dynasty
Frum: Torah-observant in daily life
Galut: Exile
Geulah: Messianic redemption

Gut Shabbos: Good Sabbath
Hachlata: Resolution one makes for the sake of self-improvement
Hachnasat Orchim: The commandment of inviting guests into one's home
Hakadosh Baruch Hu: G-d. Lit., the Holy One, blessed be He
Hashem Yikom Damam: May G-d avenge their blood
Hashem: G-d. Lit., The Name
Hashgacha Protis: Divine Providence
Hashgacha: Kosher certification of a food product
Kabbalat Shabbat: The Friday night prayer welcoming in the Shabbat
Kaddish: Traditional prayer of remembrance for the deceased
Kallah: Bride
Kashrut: Jewish dietary laws
Kavanah: Inner intention
Kedusha: Holiness
Ketubah: Jewish legal marriage contract
Kever Rachel: Tomb of the matriarch Rachel
Kiddush: Traditional blessing recited over the wine on the Sabbath
Kiddushin: One part of the process of legal Jewish marriage
Kipa Sruga: Knitted skullcap, typically worn by Modern Orthodox Jews
Klal Yisrael: The Jewish People
Kohanim: Members of the historical priestly caste of Israel, and/or current decedents thereof
Kohen Gadol: The High Priest of the Holy Temple in Jerusalem
Korbanot: The ritual offerings (animals) brought to the Holy Temple in Jerusalem to be sacrificed
Kotel: The Western Wall in Jerusalem
Kriat Yam Suf: The splitting of the Red Sea
Kvitzus Haderech: The supernatural capacity to instantaneously traverse any distance
Lashon Hara: Slanderous talk; gossip
Lecha Dodi: Sabbath prayer recited during Friday night prayer service
Levayah: Funeral
Ma Rabu Maasecha Hashem: "How great and many are your creations, O L-rd!"
Maggid of Mezrich: Rabbi Dov-Ber, successor of the Baal Shem Tov

Manna: The miraculous source of sustenance given by G-d to the Israelites in the desert

Mashiach Tzidkeinu: The Messiah, our righteous redeemer

Mashiach: Messiah

Mashpia: One who helps guide another in their spiritual development

Matzah: The unleavened bread traditionally eaten on Passover

Mazel Tov: Good luck! Congratulations!

Mazel: Good fortune or luck

Mekubal: A holy individual who can help others based on Heavenly insights and deep Torah knowledge

Mentsch: A person of admirable character; an upright, responsible individual

Mesirat Nefesh: Fervent dedication in the fulfillment of a holy task; self-sacrifice

Metapelet: Nanny

Mezuzah: An encased parchment with specific verses written on it by a certified scribe, traditionally affixed to the doorposts in a Jewish home

Mi K'Amcha Yisrael: "No nation is comparable to thee, O Israel!"

Middah K'neged Middah: Measure for measure

Midrash: Classic body of Jewish Rabbinic texts

Mikdash M'aat: Miniature temple. Can refer either to one's body, which should be respected and kept holy, or to one's home, which should be a holy structure like the Holy Temple in Jerusalem

Mikvah: A ritual bath; immersion in a Mikvah renders one spiritually purified

Mincha: The daily afternoon prayer

Minyan: A quorum of ten Jewish males assembled for prayer

Mishnah: An early written compilation of Jewish oral tradition, the basis of the Talmud

Mitnagdim: Jews who oppose Chassidism

Mitzvah Goreret Mitzvah: „One good deed leads to another."

Mitzvot: The 613 Jewish Commandments

Moshe: Moses

Motzaei Shabbat: The period following sundown on Saturday; when Shabbos departs

Nachas: A distinct feeling characterized by a combination of pride and joy

Nachshon Ben Aminadav: A prince of the tribe of Judah; the brother-in-law of Aaron the high priest; an exceptionally courageous and non-conformist person
Nashim Tzidkoniot: Righteous women throughout Jewish history
Naviah: A prophetess
Neshama Klali: The collective Jewish soul
Neshama: Soul
Ohel: The Rebbe's burial place; lit., tent
Olam Habah: The World to come
Parnasah: Livelihood
Pasuk: An individual verse from the Torah
Pesach: Passover
Pintele Yid: The irreducible element of one's Jewish identity
Pushkas: Charity box
Rabbi Elozor Ben Azaria: First-century Mishnaic sage
Rabbi Manis Friedman: Internationally renowned lecturer and author of the acclaimed *Doesn't Anyone Blush Anymore?*
Rabbi Meir Lau: Former Ashkenazi Chief Rabbi of the State of Israel
Rabbi Menachem Mendel Schneerson: Seventh Rebbe in the Chabad-Lubavitch dynasty
Ramban: Rabbi Moshe ben Nachman, prolific medieval Jewish scholar
Rashbi: Acronym for Rabbi Shimon Bar Yochai
Rashi: Rabbi Shlomo Yitzchaki, prolific medieval Jewish scholar, most famous for his commentary on the Bible and Talmud
Rav: An expert in all matters pertaining to the interpretation and/or application of Jewish Law
Rebbe Rashab: Rabbi Sholom Dov-Ber Schneerson, the fifth Rebbe of the Chabad dynasty
Rebbe: A Chassidic Master; can also refer to the leader of a particular Chassidic dynasty, e.g. "the Lubavitcher Rebbe"
Rebbetzin Chana: Mother of the 7th Lubavitcher Rebbe, Rabbi Menachem Mendel Schneerson.
Refuah Shleimah: Speedy recovery
Rivkah: The matriarch Rebecca
Sarah Imeinu: Our matriarch Sarah
Sefer Torah: A Torah scroll
Sefer: Book
Segulot: Holy remedies which can be recited in times of need
Seudah: Feast

Shabbat, Shabbos: The Jewish Sabbath, which begins Friday night and ends Saturday night
Shabtai Tzvi: Pseudo-messiah in Jewish history
Shacharit: The daily morning prayer
Shadchan: A matchmaker
Shalom: Peace
Shechina: The feminine dimension of the Divine.
Shehechiyanu: A traditional blessing of renewal recited on holidays and other special occasions
Shidduch: A potential suitor for marriage, or an idea for one
Shiva: Week-long period of mourning for an immediate family member
Shliach: An emissary of the Lubavitcher Rebbe
Shlomo Hamelech: King Solomon
Shluchim/Shluchot: Male/Female emissaries of the Lubavitcher Rebbe
Shmatte: Rag
Sholom Aleichem: The prayer sung on Friday nights at the table, right before the Sabbath meal.
Shomer Mitzvot: One who observes the commandments
Shtetl: One of many small towns in Eastern Europe which had a significant Jewish population in the centuries preceding to the Holocaust
Shul: Synagogue
Shulchan Aruch: The Code of Jewish Law
Siddur: Prayer book
Simcha Poretz Geder: Joy breaks through any barrier
Simcha: Happiness, or a happy occasion such as a wedding, Bar/Bat Mitzvah, or Brit Milah.
Sofer: A professional scribe
Tahara: the quality of ritual purity
Taharat Hamishpacha: Family Purity; the Jewish Laws pertaining to sexual relations between husband and wife
Talmid Chochom: A Torah scholar
Talmud Torah: A Jewish primary school
Tanach: Acronym for Torah, Nevi'im, Ketuvim
Tanya: The magnum opus of Rabbi Shneur Zalman of Liadi, also known as the Alter Rebbe, first leader of the Chabad dynasty
Tefillin: Phylacteries worn by Jewish men during daily morning prayers
Tehillim: Psalms

Tevye and Golda: Protagonists of Sholom Aleichem's *Tevye the Dairyman*, the book which later inspired the famous film "Fiddler on the Roof"
Tisha B'av: Day of commemoration for the destruction of both the First and Second Temples in Jerusalem.
Torah: The Five Books of Moses
Tzaddik: A righteous individual; in Chabad philosophy, one who has attained the loftiest level of spiritual development.
Tzedaka: The mitzvah to give charity
Tzitzit: Ritual fringed garment worn by Jewish males
Yaakov: The patriarch Jacob
Yahrzeit: The traditional commemoration on the date of someone's passing
Yaldah: Girl
Yarmulke: Head covering for Jewish males
Yechidus: Private audience with a Rebbe
Yemach Shemo: "May his [an evil individual's] name be expunged"
Yerushalayim: Jerusalem
Yeshiva: An institution for Jewish learning
Yidden: Jews
Yiddish: The nearly 1,000-year-old language of Ashkenazic Jewry
Yiddishe Kinderlach: Jewish children
Yiddishkeit: Lit. "Jewishness"
Yirat Shamayim: Fear of Heaven
Yitzchak: The patriarch Isaac
Yom Kippur: The annual Day of Atonement
Zemirot: Traditional Jewish songs
Zchut: Merit